ASSERTIVENESS WORKBOOK

ASSERTIVENESS WORKBOOK

Practical Exercises to Improve Communication, Set Boundaries, and Be Your Best Advocate

Shandelle Hether-Gray, MA, LMHC

ROCKRIDGE
PRESS

CONTENTS

INTRODUCTION AND HOW TO USE THIS BOOK

Welcome! If you're reading this, chances are you struggle with communication, setting boundaries, and standing up for yourself—and that's okay. This struggle can vary from person to person or situation to situation. It might look like difficulty saying no to a partner or friend, or heavy use of sarcasm to express your feelings. It could be struggling to ask a medical professional for a second opinion, or holding back from making new friends.

More people struggle with asserting themselves than we might realize, and it's understandable. We don't take classes on this stuff in our formative years. It's likely that no one pulled you aside in middle school for a workshop on how to assert yourself and express your thoughts, feelings, wants, and needs. If this did happen to you, though, kudos to you and your A+ school! This book will teach you the skills needed to be your own best advocate and to assert yourself. It can also be used by mental health professionals working with clients to cultivate assertiveness skills.

My name is Shandelle, and I am a mental health counselor who helps people of all ages learn to communicate better and build the relationships and lives they want. I help my clients understand that the way they communicate and even the way they *think* is strongly tied to their past experiences, including upbringing and cultural experiences. I also show them how their current style of communicating can be improved to better serve them.

This book is meant to be a succinct, practical introduction to assertiveness. Chapter 1 will provide you with information about different communication styles, give you insight into your communication patterns (especially in times of conflict), help you identify your barriers to assertive communication, and review the plentiful benefits of being a skilled and assertive communicator. Chapter 2 focuses on the "how to," discussing the key components of assertiveness and providing you with important tips and strategies. Chapters 3 through 6 address how assertive needs and their practical execution may vary depending on the setting or situation. Each chapter includes exercises to help you challenge your current communication style, build your assertiveness skills, and practice the techniques discussed.

Practice is key when learning any new skill. It determines how successful you will ultimately be in executing the skill on your own, even when you're in a state of crisis. For example, you could read about infant CPR and feel you understand the gist of it, but, in the unfortunate event that you actually need to perform it, wouldn't you feel a whole lot more confident if you had practiced it beforehand? I want you to feel confident asserting yourself, not just understanding the theory behind it.

Let's get to work!

CHAPTER ONE

THE BENEFITS OF BEING ASSERTIVE

Take a minute and think about how effectively you communicate your needs. Do you feel satisfied with the conversations you have, or do you often leave them feeling dejected, unheard, disrespected, or angry? How would you characterize your typical communication style? Are you able to get most of your needs met in your interactions with others? How would you benefit from adopting an assertive communication style?

    This chapter will help you address these important questions. It will cover what healthy and unhealthy communication look like, and you'll get an in-depth look at different communication styles. Read through the activity starting on page 2 to help you identify your communication patterns. And it's okay if you don't feel quite ready to change! Review the possible benefits of working on your communication style anyway. You might get more comfortable with adopting some of these techniques over time.

What Is Communication?

Communication is the transmission of information from one person to another. It can occur verbally, in writing, through body language, or by other means, such as sign language. Whatever method you use, your ability to communicate is vitally important. It allows you to express yourself; share your thoughts, values, and feelings; demonstrate your needs and desires; and build healthy relationships.

Healthy communication is honest and direct. It allows you to advocate for yourself while respecting the rights and boundaries of others. It is flexible and determined by the context or situation. Unhealthy communication is generally the opposite of these things. It can look like holding back and not speaking up, or talking but not communicating what you honestly think or need. Unhealthy communication can be emotional or even explosive. It can sound like blaming—creating a breeding ground for defensiveness in conversations, rather than an open dialogue. Additionally, the way we communicate with ourselves—our inner voice, which reflects our beliefs about our abilities and our past experiences—strongly influences how we communicate with others.

Four communication styles exist on a continuum: passive, aggressive, passive-aggressive, and assertive. While people might engage heavily in one style of communication, it is important to note that communication style is not fixed. A person may demonstrate different styles at different times or in different situations. Each of these styles differs in its degree of directness, self-advocacy, respectfulness of boundaries, and likelihood of meeting needs.

What's My Communication Style?

Consider the following scenario: After years of working, budgeting your spending, and saving your money, you are finally able to buy your dream home. Soon after you have unpacked your furniture and had a chance to put your feet up, your new neighbors move in. They seem like fine neighbors at first, until one day you notice that they are planting a row of apple trees between their property and yours. You realize that the trees are, in fact, planted well onto your property. This upsets you, and you want to discuss the issue with your neighbors.

Which of the following statements most accurately describes how you would address this conflict?

a. You ask your neighbors to meet. When you are face-to-face, you feel bad about addressing the issue. You assume that surely they didn't know that they were planting on your property. You may worry that saying something could cause them to react poorly and result in a negative long-term relationship. So you say nothing, and nothing changes. The trees grow very large over the years, and each autumn you are left to pick up rotting apples from your yard before the mice, rabbits, and birds arrive. The situation is so infuriating and depressing that you consider moving.

b. You dig up the trees and drag them to your neighbors' porch, where you tell them that they should have looked at the property lines before planting. You may throw in an insult or threaten that if they do anything like this again, you will go to the homeowners' association or get a lawyer. Your neighbors are angry to see their hard work undone and to find that some of their trees were damaged in the uprooting. The rest of the time you spend as neighbors is contentious, filled with disputes and subtle attacks.

c. You see your neighbors in the grocery store and start chatting. Frustrated by the trees on your property, you make a sarcastic comment that they must be quitting their jobs and running an orchard, because there is no other reason they would plant so many trees. You say that your yard looks a whole lot smaller now, and hope that they bring up the issue of property lines. They don't, so you leave the conversation frustrated, vowing not to invite them to your holiday party.

d. You arrange a meeting with your neighbors. You acknowledge the hard work they have done planting and ask them about their plans for their yard. You kindly bring up the issue of property lines, telling them that, unfortunately, their trees are on your side of the property. You request that they move the trees. They express embarrassment and tell you that they had no idea they had planted on your property. They agree to move the trees.

Passive

If you answered (a), you might have a tendency toward passive communication. A person who communicates passively tends to avoid expressing their thoughts or feelings, especially when they might conflict with others. They may think they are being respectful of others by not speaking up for themselves, but this passivity robs them of their ability to advocate for themselves and meet their own needs. This self-denial may lead to feelings of anxiety, helplessness, and resentment.

Passive communicators may also:

Go along with what others want.

Agree to the requests of others, even when they don't want to.

Believe they are weak or that people walk all over them.

Have difficulty making eye contact.

Benefits:

- They may avoid the temporary discomfort of conflict and believe they are pre-serving relationships.

Drawbacks:

- Others do not know what the passive person needs or wants.

- They may be less likely to get their needs met.

- They are likely to feel frustrated and ineffective in their communication.

- They are likely to "bottle up" their emotions until the strain becomes too much. They then express themselves in unregulated or out-of-control ways that leave them feeling guilty or with unintended consequences, such as hurting others. This cycle only confirms their belief that they cannot stand up for themselves, reinforcing the pattern of passivity.

Aggressive

Answer (b) is an example of an aggressive communication style. Individuals with an aggressive style communicate directly about their thoughts, values, and feelings. They have no problem advocating for themselves. However, they may be disrespectful of others' rights and boundaries, often violating boundaries to meet their needs.

Aggressive communicators may also:

Use threats and intimidation to get what they need or want.

Blame others or use "you statements," escalating the conflict.

Speak loudly.

Readily express anger or frustration.

Think or say things like "How dare you do this to me?"

Benefits:

- They may be likely to get their needs met.

Drawbacks:

- Their tendency to violate others' rights to meet their own needs often results in poor relationships with others.

- They may feel guilt over their aggressiveness.

Passive-Aggressive

As demonstrated by answer (c), a person with a passive-aggressive communication style communicates indirectly about their thoughts and feelings, often through sarcasm, body language, or actions. They have difficulty advocating for themselves. Their indirect attempts to communicate their thoughts and feelings often cross others' boundaries or violate their right to respect.

Passive-aggressive communicators may also:

Hint at how they feel or what they want.

Retaliate or sabotage others whom they feel disagree with them.

Use phrases such as "I guess that's okay" or "If you really want to."

Make inconsistent facial expressions, such as smiling when annoyed or not making eye contact.

Mumble or talk under their breath.

Benefits:

• Others might get their indirect message, so the passive-aggressive person does not need to directly confront them.

Drawbacks:

• They are less likely to get their needs met due to not directly expressing their needs or feelings.

• Feelings of frustration and anger are likely outcomes for all parties.

• Relationships will likely suffer due to this communication style.

Assertive

Answer (d) demonstrates how an assertive person might respond to their neighbors. Assertive communication directly expresses the thoughts, values, and feelings of an individual without violating the rights and boundaries of others or being disrespectful. The assertive person firmly advocates for themselves and is comfortable making requests of others.

In our example, the neighbors agree to the assertive communicator's request and their needs are met. This isn't a guarantee; the neighbors might have refused to move the trees. In this case, the individual would need to further advocate for their needs, make an additional request, or initiate legal action.

The assertive communicator also:

Comfortably makes eye contact.

Speaks clearly and honestly.

Says no comfortably.

Uses "I statements" to own their thoughts and feelings.

Is unapologetic in expressing their needs and feelings.

Is willing to compromise with others when appropriate.

Benefits:

- Assertive people are more likely to get their needs met.

- They are more likely to have healthy relationships.

- They have a greater sense of autonomy in their life.

- They are able to say no, so they are less likely to overextend themselves.

Why Am I Not Assertive? Factors That Contribute to Your Communication Style

As a therapist trained in cognitive behavioral therapy (CBT), I try to focus on the here and now with my clients. If people dive too much into the past, they can easily get stuck there, wasting today's opportunities. However, when a person's past experiences and mis-learnings directly interfere with their ability to reach their goals today, this must be addressed.

Our past is only one roadblock to asserting ourselves. Others include our gender, race, cultural identity and experiences, personality traits, and psychological health. It is important to recognize your individual roadblocks so you can navigate them and enjoy a smoother ride through life. The following list of common roadblocks is not exhaustive; look for the ones that apply to you.

Background and History

It might be tempting to think that your difficulty with assertiveness is innate or something you acquired at birth. However, it is actually something you have learned throughout your life. Operational learning theory suggests that our communication style is determined by how others or our environment responded to our communication attempts. You were either rewarded or punished for the way you communicated, influencing your future communication style.

For example, imagine a little boy at a birthday party. He wants a piece of cake, but he is too shy to ask for one. His older brother sees him in front of the cake and asks the adult for a slice for his little brother. The boy was rewarded—given something he wanted—for not asking for what he wanted. This situation might have implicitly taught him that he doesn't need to speak up, because others identify—and will meet—his needs. This could lead him to develop a more passive style of communication.

Here's another example: A kindergarten-age girl on the playground asks her teacher if she can use the bathroom. The teacher says no, and the girl wets herself. As you can imagine, this is quite an embarrassing situation for a kid. She was punished for being assertive, receiving not only the undesirable consequence of not being allowed to use the bathroom when she needed to, but also suffering the embarrassment and potential teasing from classmates. This experience might contribute to a constellation of beliefs: that she is incapable of standing up for herself or getting what she needs, or that others are cruel or unfair. She may feel discomfort about asking for what she wants and needs in the future.

While we learn much from our own rewards and punishments, social learning theory suggests that we also learn through observing the rewards and punishments received by others. If we observe someone getting a reward for asserting themselves—either by getting what they want/need or by receiving praise or another reward for their assertion—then we are likely to emulate this behavior in similar future situations. If instead we observe someone who is punished, criticized, or not getting their wants/needs met for asserting themselves, then we are less likely to copy their behavior.

Our personal history is full of opportunities for mis-learning communication. This is our first roadblock to being an assertive communicator.

Gender

Men and women generally have different expectations for their communication styles based on societal stereotypes of supposed feminine and masculine characteristics. For women in the United States, socially desirable—and thus more feminine—traits have traditionally included being "affectionate, cheerful, compassionate," communal, and "sensitive to the needs of others"; "eager to soothe hurt feelings"; and "gentle, shy, soft-spoken, understanding," and "yielding." Traits deemed more desirable in men— and hence more masculine—include being "aggressive, assertive, competitive," and "dominant"; acting as a leader; defending one's own beliefs; taking a stand; and being "independent" and "self-sufficient."[1]

These traits are consistent with the traditional ways boys and girls are socialized and raised. Boys are often encouraged to be independent, play rough, and engage in sports or active play. Girls have traditionally been encouraged to be more social, value physical appearance, and use imaginative play.

Research has historically supported the notion that boys are more assertive than girls, and this is evident even in preschool-age children.[2] This doesn't mean that girls aren't or can't be assertive. *They absolutely can!* However, since aggression and assertiveness are considered more "masculine," when a woman exhibits these traits, others might be surprised and label her as hostile, bossy, or bitchy.[3] I don't mean to imply that boys are always assertive. Anyone can struggle with assertiveness. The research simply points to the tendency for boys to be more assertive and to appear more assertive to others.

It is easy to see how stereotypes, along with differential socialization, affect communication. If you receive messages that you are supposed to be dominant, independent, decisive, and self-sufficient, and you have more experience with a type of socialization that fosters these traits, then you will learn to communicate with more confidence. You will speak more directly and more readily advocate for yourself. If you are instead told that you should be gentle, shy, yielding, and eager to soothe hurt feelings, and you are socialized to prioritize social or community needs over your own, research shows that you will be less confident in speaking up for yourself and less likely to communicate directly.

Among children, girls are found to be more talkative and to express emotions more in their speech, while boys tend to use more assertive speech.[4] Even as adults, women use more hedging language—words that express vagueness or uncertainty, like "maybe" or "kind of." They elaborate more in their speech, speaking in longer sentences and using intensifying adverbs, like "very" or "really." They also refer to emotions more often.[5]

Whether you identify as male, female, or non-binary, there is no denying that gender stereotypes, gendered socialization, and gender role modeling have influenced your communication in some way, so be on the lookout for this potential roadblock. In chapter 3, we will discuss how gender adds challenges when asserting yourself in the workplace.

Culture

Your culture and the culture of those you interact with influences your communication style and can contribute to miscommunications and unintended conflict.

Cross-cultural research on assertiveness indicates that assertiveness is valued differently in individualistic and collectivistic cultures. Individualistic or Western societies, like the United States and Australia, emphasize the importance of independence, personal goals, and agency, and assertiveness is thus highly valued in these cultures. Collectivism, which dominates in Asian or Eastern cultures, places greater importance on the group and community needs, and as such does not value assertiveness.[6] In fact,

Asian cultures may prefer more subtle and indirect language[7] and interpret the direct nature of Western assertiveness as disrespectful.

Directness is only one feature of assertive communication, as you will read about in chapter 2. Other features of this communication style include nonverbal behavior, such as eye contact, posture, physical proximity of the people conversing, and volume of speech. These nonverbal behaviors also vary by culture and are important to understand to prevent miscommunication. People from a collectivistic culture are more likely to demonstrate minimal eye contact out of respect, stand close to the person they are talking to, and speak more quietly.[8] If you are from the United States talking to someone from an Asian culture, and you are unaware of these nonverbal differences, you might interpret the person you're speaking to as meek, shy, or rude.

Although delving deeper into cultural influences is outside the scope of this book, it is worth noting that the impact of culture is not as simple as research on individualism and collectivism might suggest. For example, individuals who are Middle Eastern are considered part of a collectivistic culture, but they have demonstrated assertiveness similar to that of Westerners.[9] Differences in assertiveness are also seen within cultures. For example, students in New York demonstrate more assertiveness than students in the Midwestern regions of the United States.[10]

Race

Outside of some research from the 1980s and 1990s, much of the research on assertive communication focuses on white people. Among white people in the US, especially white men, assertiveness and self-advocacy are valued positively. Despite a paucity of research on racial differences regarding assertiveness, it seems colloquially that an individual's race influences their communication style through a number of factors. These include values and expectations from and among group members, stereotypes from other racial groups that influence perceptions of assertive behavior, and the real-life consequences or feared consequences of assertive communication. Let's consider some examples.

Among some in Asian cultures who place a high value on community and offering deference to others, advocating for one's own needs over the needs of others may come across as abrasive and disrespectful. When interacting with different racial groups with differing perceptions and values on assertiveness, however, this same approach may help them meet their needs.

Similarly, some BIPOC (Black, Indigenous, people of color) may feel more comfortable asserting themselves to others in their racial community than to those outside of it. Issues of systemic racism and discrimination may influence whether they feel safe using this same assertive communication style with others, especially to others in roles of authority.

Therapists using this workbook with clients should take into consideration each client's racial and ethnic background and their goals for communication when adapting the skills outlined in this book. If you are working through this book on your own, keep in mind how you may need to adapt the skills to fit your needs.

Anxiety

Anxiety, particularly social anxiety, has long been associated with assertiveness difficulties.[11] Anxiety is a significant roadblock to assertiveness for most of my clients. Regardless of whether you suffer from clinical anxiety, the idea of self-advocating or expressing conflict can be uncomfortable, and this often leads to passivity and avoidance.

Repeat after me: *The more you avoid something that makes you feel anxious, the worse your anxiety about that thing will become.*

Our anxiety about assertion is usually based on irrational or fear-based beliefs that we developed from our past about ourselves, others, and our world, such as:

"If I tell people how I feel, they will use it against me."

"If I say no, my boss will think I can't handle the work."

"I'm inadequate."

"My friends will think I am too sensitive if I tell them that their comment hurt me."

"I don't want to be rude or make people uncomfortable."

We need to challenge these anxiety-producing beliefs, and one way to do this is through exposure to practicing assertiveness. As reviewed by Speed, Goldstein, and Goldfried, assertiveness training programs have been shown to reduce anxiety as well as other forms of psychological distress, and they may even be as effective as the evidence-based treatment cognitive behavioral therapy.[12]

Other Factors

Personality. An individual's personality also seems to influence their level of assertiveness. Cross-culturally, assertiveness has been shown to correspond to two of the Big Five personality traits: neuroticism (characterized by emotional instability, anxiety, anger, and insecurity) and extraversion (characterized by sociability, activeness, and outgoingness). This research has found higher levels of assertiveness among people who score low on measures of neuroticism and high on extraversion.[13]

Self-esteem. Self-esteem refers to a person's view of their value and self-worth. Passive communication styles have been correlated with low self-esteem.[14]

Situation. Situational factors may also prove to be roadblocks to assertiveness. For example, a recent study sought to teach assertiveness skills to Hispanic and non-Hispanic construction workers in hopes that it would help them speak up about on-the-job safety issues and result in fewer injuries. They found that participants chose not to practice assertiveness skills at work, perhaps due to the belief that it would negatively impact their employment.[15]

Assertiveness Is a Style

Assertiveness refers to a social skill and a style of communicating. It is not a value judgment about a person. Think about it: Would you say that a person who has difficulties with public speaking is a bad or "weak" person? No! They just haven't mastered the skill of public speaking. You are not a bad or weak person if you are not assertive; you just need to build up your communication skills.

Also, keep in mind that no one is assertive 100 percent of the time. It may not even be safe or appropriate in every situation. For example, if you are in an abusive relationship or are the victim of domestic violence, it might not be safe for you to practice assertiveness. Additionally, the adage of the "right time and place" is important to keep in mind. While it might be good to give your boss constructive feedback or bring up a source of on-the-job conflict, it may not be appropriate to do so in front of your colleagues. Similarly, being more passive or aggressive in a situation might be warranted. If you are dealing with a person you know will not listen to you, then you might decide to communicate more passively, rather than wasting your effort trying to talk to them. If you encounter a person who continues to cross your boundaries despite your assertiveness, you might need to escalate to being more aggressive. Keep in mind that aggressiveness does not equal violence; it might manifest as taking a firmer stance or raising your voice to get their attention.

You Are in Charge of Yourself

Being assertive is about showing up for yourself, respecting yourself, and taking ownership and control of your emotions, thoughts, and behavior. You may have heard the airplane metaphor about the importance of putting your own oxygen mask on and meeting your needs first so that you are better able to help others.

Remember, You Can't Control Others

Asserting yourself is not about changing other people or making them do what you want them to do. Everyone has the right of autonomy; we cannot control anyone else, and nor should we try. However, when a person's views or behaviors directly affect you negatively, you have the right to assert yourself and let them know. They might not be aware of their impact on you; telling them will help them understand and potentially change their behavior. On the other hand, they might know and not care that what they're doing has an impact on you. Knowing this might help you decide how much of a role this person should play in your life.

Your Needs May Not Always Be Met

You can be a master of assertiveness and still not always get your needs met. Remember, you can't control others. They have a right to their needs, which may not always be compatible with yours. Asserting yourself, however, will allow you to communicate more effectively, increasing the chances of getting your needs met.

Why Be Assertive?

Change takes work. Changing your communication style and learning to assert yourself require effort, and you are going to need to practice the skills outlined in this book. But here is the thing: *The practice is going to be worth it*.

If you are voluntarily reading this book, you probably want to change and are ready to put in the work. Be aware that in the initial stages of changing and practicing assertiveness, it is normal to feel a slight increase in stress and discomfort. You are trying something new and challenging—adjusting your patterns of passivity, aggression, or passive aggression that allowed you to avoid stress, but not to meet your wants or needs. Think of it like quitting smoking or modifying any other habit. The first few days after you make the change, you might feel agitated and crave the old habit, but as time goes on you will feel better.

Asserting yourself will get easier, too. If you need more convincing, consider these reasons for adopting an assertive communication style:

More equal relationships. Assertiveness training will help you better communicate your needs and wants to your partner. You will be more willing to discuss them and feel more confident and comfortable when you do.

You deserve nice things. Maybe you were taught to minimize your needs and focus on the needs of others. Other people are important, but you should be the main character in the book of your life. You deserve to be happy and fulfilled.

Assertiveness as a social skill. You owe it to yourself and your personal growth to develop this social skill, as it will help you achieve most of your life goals.

If you don't advocate for yourself, no one else will. No one knows you as well as you know yourself or is as well-equipped to advocate on your behalf. Getting more comfortable using your voice will help you get what you know you want or need instead of what others might assume you want or need.

The Research

Roadblocks don't have to stop you! Assertiveness training can help you, regardless of your personal roadblocks. Training programs to improve assertiveness skills have been shown to reduce anxiety and other forms of psychological distress,[16, 17, 18] improve self-esteem,[19] improve relationship satisfaction,[20] and improve academic performance,[21] regardless of gender, culture, and personality type.[22, 23] Begin your skills training now by going through the exercises listed throughout this book.

EXERCISES

1. What's Your Communication Style?

Reflect on the last conflict you had with a friend or a coworker. Which of the communication styles in this chapter (see page 2) matches how you responded to this conflict? In what way did your communication style influence the outcome of the conflict? How could you have responded differently?

....

....

....

....

....

....

....

....

2. Who Is Your Assertiveness Role Model?

Think of someone you know whom you consider an assertive communicator. You might know them personally, or they could be someone famous. How do you know they are effective at this style of communication? Describe how they might use their body language to help them communicate assertively.

....

....

....

....

....

....

....

....

....

....

3. Where Did You Learn It?

Think about your personal history and what you read about operational learning theory (see page 6). Identify three situations in which you might have learned not to assert yourself. In each of these situations, how was your communication style rewarded or punished? These situations do not need to be limited to childhood; feel free to include recent situations.

SITUATION	REWARD/PUNISHMENT	EFFECT ON YOUR COMMUNICATION
1.		
2.		
3.		

4. Cognitive Roadblocks

Imagine that you are in a situation where assertiveness is needed or you want to assert yourself. What thoughts seem to jump into your mind to stop you? If you have a hard time eliciting these thoughts, try these sentence completions:

I ....

....

If ....

...., then

....

....

....

....

....

....

....

....

....

....

5. Gender Restrictions

What messages did you receive growing up about how you were supposed to act or communicate based on your gender? How did you feel about those messages? Did you accept them or fight against them? How might those messages have influenced how others saw you?

6. Assertiveness and Flexibility

Remember that assertiveness is not an approach that should be practiced 100 percent of the time. What is one situation in your life where a passive communication style might actually be more useful?

....

....

....

....

7. Culture

What, if any, messages have you received from your culture about the value of assertiveness—for people in general, people of your identified gender, etc.?

....

....

....

....

....

....

....

....

....

8. Impact on Others: Part One

Do you think the people close to you want you to be more assertive? Why or why not?

_____

_____

_____

_____

_____

_____

_____

Part Two: Test Your Hypothesis!

Ask a friend/family member if they want you to be more assertive, or think you have a problem with assertiveness. Did their response surprise you? How might their response influence your motivation to enhance your assertiveness skills?

_____

_____

_____

_____

_____

_____

_____

9. Decide to Change

What are the pros and cons of changing your current communication style?

PROS	CONS

10. What Have You Lost? What Could You Gain?

What have you lost by your current style of passivity, aggression, or passive aggression? What do you hope to gain by becoming more assertive?

Losses:

....

....

....

....

....

Anticipated Gains:

....

....

....

....

....

....

CHAPTER TWO

HOW TO BE ASSERTIVE

Now let's get into the nitty-gritty of *how* to be assertive. I'm going to show you what asserting yourself with confidence looks like and explain to you why it is important to practice the strategies discussed here, even if you aren't feeling confident yet. Don't know what things to assert yourself on, or where to start practicing? This chapter will help you identify your wants and needs, and how to use assertiveness skills to obtain them.

Fake It 'Til You ~~Make~~ Become It: Projecting Assertiveness

Have you ever felt nervous about doing something, like giving a presentation, and tried to psych yourself up by telling yourself that you can do it, you are prepared, and it will all work out? If so, what you might have done next was go into the presentation, stand tall, smile at the audience, and say what you came to say. Instead of showing your nervousness, you projected confidence. This is called "faking it," and research shows that it indeed can help us feel more confident and able.

Researchers from Columbia and Harvard University have demonstrated that faking even brief nonverbal displays of power, called power poses, can make us feel and act more powerful by impacting our hormones and subsequent actions. In their research, Carney, Cuddy, and Yap randomly assigned a sample of men and women to hold either a high-power pose or a low-power pose for one minute prior to completing a gambling task. Researchers took saliva samples afterward to measure participants' levels of testosterone—a hormone that, when elevated, might signal competitiveness, risk-taking, and dominance—and the stress hormone cortisol. Their results suggested that the group who "faked it" by practicing the high-power pose had higher levels of testosterone and lower cortisol, described feeling more powerful, and took more risks than the participants who were asked to hold the low-power pose.[24]

Faking assertiveness doesn't only help us *appear* more assertive to others. If we continue to practice it and challenge our own individual roadblocks (discussed in chapter 1; see page 6), we can fine-tune our assertive communication skills and actually *become* more assertive.

So how do you fake it? You need to demonstrate assertive body language, practice assertive listening, and know what to say—or at least have some assertive verbal phrases at the ready to guide you.

Assertive Body Language

You communicate your thoughts, feelings, wants, or needs only partly through the words you use, or your verbal communication. The way you use your body when you are engaged in communication, called body language or nonverbal communication, also plays a major role in what you convey to others. If a picture is worth a thousand words, your body is the picture that gives the words you use context, telling the observer how accurate your words are and how serious you are.

Imagine seeing your coworker in the hallway. You ask him how he is, and he says, "I'm okay." This phrase rapidly changes meaning based on the body language that accompanies it.

- "I'm okay" + neutral posture and facial expression ⟶ coworker feels okay

- "I'm okay" + staring down at the floor, tearful, arms crossed ⟶ coworker is upset

- "I'm okay" + labored breathing, clutching chest ⟶ coworker might be having a medical emergency

In the first situation, your coworker's verbal communication is consistent with their body language, and their message is clear. There is inconsistency in the next two situations between what is being said and what you are observing, which leads you to question your coworker's statement and puts you in the difficult position of guessing what they mean.

You don't want people to guess at what you mean or think you are not serious when you assert yourself. Striving for consistency between your words and your body language will result in clear and unambiguous communication. Here are some guidelines for assertive body language.

1. Try to maintain comfortable eye contact when talking and listening to others, including periodic breaks or glances around the room. Avoid a gaze that is too rigid, which might come across as aggressively "staring down," but don't take too many breaks in eye contact to avoid appearing uninterested or uncomfortable.

2. Facial expressions should match the emotional tone of your message and your verbal communication. While it is okay to express negative emotions, try to avoid strong displays of them, as this could overshadow your message and make the other person less likely to respond positively to you.

3. Pay attention to your posture. Your posture tells people how comfortable you are and whether you are interested in talking to them. Assertive posture is characterized by standing up straight but comfortably, not slouched. Your body should be angled toward the person you are talking to.

4. Your arms and hands should be relaxed, either at your sides or in another position that feels appropriate for the situation, such as holding an object. Avoid arms crossed in front of you, which can communicate defiance or discomfort. Hands should also not be in pockets or fidgeting, as this could suggest disinterest, boredom, or distraction.

5. Your voice should be steady and appropriate in volume, neither too quiet nor too loud. The emotional tone should be respectful and consistent with that of your message. Avoid lengthy speech or monologues, and strive for a back-and-forth dialogue.

See the Communication Styles and Body Language table for a summary of assertive body language, as well as some contrasting ways that your body can communicate passivity and aggression. If you notice yourself displaying some of these passive or aggressive behaviors, be mindful of this and try to practice more assertive behaviors instead.

COMMUNICATION STYLES AND BODY LANGUAGE

	PASSIVE	ASSERTIVE	AGGRESSIVE
Eye Contact	Indirect; fleeting or brief; avoidant	Direct with natural breaks or shifts	Direct; may be intense and doesn't break or shift naturally
Facial Expression	May express inconsistent emotions, like smiling when talking about something unpleasant	Consistent with emotional tone of message	May express anger, annoyance, or disdain
Posture	Hunched over to make your body smaller; body angled or facing slightly away from the person you are speaking to	Standing straight; your body facing the person you are speaking with at a comfortable distance away that respects personal space	Standing tall or taking up a lot of space; your body facing the other person, but may be standing too close as a means of intimidation

Arms and Hands	Arms may be crossed in front of your body; hands in pockets, behind you, or fidgeting with objects	Arms and hands comfortably at your sides; hand gestures may be used to emphasize verbal points	Muscles in arms may appear tense; hands may be clenched out of anger or for intimidation
Voice	Voice may be shaky; tone could reflect uncertainty, or be noncommittal or overly agreeable; volume might seem low; length may be either too short or too lengthy and apologetic	Steady, emotionally neutral tone; volume appropriate to situation; speech is direct and not too lengthy, giving the other person opportunities to speak and have a back-and-forth flow	Tone may be sarcastic or rude; loud in volume; speech may be pressured; length of speech may be too long as a way of dominating the conversation or not giving the other person time to speak

Assertive Listening

Assertive listening is a necessary component of assertive communication. Listening first ensures that you don't miss out on important information. It also allows the parties involved to feel heard and respected. This makes conversations more pleasant and can also make people feel comfortable and more inclined to share. Assertive listening requires that you both listen attentively and show the other person that you are listening.

You may be paying attention to someone and hearing what they say, but if you look off into space while they are talking or turn your back to them, you may communicate disrespect or lack of interest, having a negative impact on the conversation. Show you're listening by maintaining comfortable eye contact, using gestures like nodding your head and smiling, asking for clarification if needed, and paraphrasing what they said.

Have Helpful Phrases at the Ready

As I've mentioned before, when you're first learning and practicing asserting yourself, you might feel uncomfortable. Having a few assertive phrases in your back pocket can help guide these initial interactions. I recommend practicing them in the mirror so you can watch your body language and adjust it as needed, to make sure your verbal and nonverbal messages are consistent. Here are some examples of helpful phrases:

"That doesn't work for me."

"I am not comfortable with that."

"I have a different opinion on this."

An "I statement" is a structured way to help you communicate your thoughts and feelings, express how someone else's actions affect you, or make a request. An "I statement" allows you to take ownership of your emotions, rather than projecting them on to others. This reduces the chance of using language that comes across as blaming or aggressive. The formula for an "I statement" is as follows:

"I feel _____

_____

when you _____

_____."

"I would appreciate it if you/Could you _____

_____."

For example: "I feel angry when you leave your clothes on the floor. Could you please put them in the hamper?"

"I'm feeling really depressed lately. I need some help getting out of the house. Can you go for a walk with me?"

"I feel upset when you say things like 'Are you an idiot?' even if you don't mean it. I would appreciate it if you didn't say things like that."

Practice

Now that you know what assertive language looks like, how it sounds (I'll discuss more about verbal assertive communication later), and how to listen assertively, *practice it*. Remember that practicing will help build your confidence and improve your communication skills. Start small. Work through the exercises in this book, then move on to real-world practice in situations where you feel safe—maybe with people you know and trust—or where the stakes are low.

Here are some guidelines to help facilitate your initial real-world practice.

1. Imagine the situation/person you want to address. Identify your intentions. Why is it important or good that you assert yourself in this situation at this time or with this person? What is the goal you hope to accomplish? This could be just practice, building your skills, increasing a partner's understanding of how you feel, etc.

2. Plan out what you want to say. Come up with a starting point or a phrase and know where you want the conversation to go. Be flexible about this, though. Remember that the other person is contributing to the conversation, too, so it is impossible to fully plan how it will go beyond your initial opening phrase.

3. Take a deep breath, stand tall, and initiate the conversation. Practice the assertive body language discussed on page 24.

4. Practice assertive listening. Be attentive. Show the other person that you are listening: Nod your head, summarize what they said, ask relevant questions.

5. Respond to what they say, if anything, and wrap up the conversation.

6. Review how you did. What did you like or dislike? What implicit or explicit feedback did you get from the other person? How could you improve your approach next time? You might be tempted to skip this step. *Don't*. Reviewing will help you fine-tune your skills and improve your practice.

Receiving and Giving Feedback

When you assert yourself, you will receive feedback from others by how they respond to you, implicitly or explicitly. Receiving this feedback thoughtfully is important. It shows you how others view your assertiveness, and if there are discrepancies between the message you intended to give and the message they received. If others receive a very different message than you think you are sending, you need to reevaluate your nonverbal behavior and your words. You can even ask them what it was about your body language or words that led them to feel/think the way they did. Asking for this kind of feedback, especially from supportive close others who know you are working to improve your assertiveness skills, can be helpful. In addition to receiving feedback, you may also want to give feedback to others.

Compliments

We generally tend to like people who like us and with whom we have positive interactions. Compliments, both given and received, are small investments we make in building positive relationships with others. It can be hard for people to accept a compliment, due to poor self-esteem, high personal standards, cultural norms, or myriad other reasons. However, being able to accept a compliment is an important part of assertiveness. Rejecting or responding poorly to a compliment projects a lack of confidence. It can also make the giver feel uncomfortable, undermining a potentially positive interaction that could have otherwise strengthened the relationship. Note that there could be some cultural differences (recall chapter 1; see page 8), where for some people accepting a compliment is considered arrogant. In that case, you may be inclined to offer or expect a different response.

Be specific when giving compliments. Try to avoid generic or short compliments, like "Nice shoes," as these aren't always considered thoughtful or genuine, and can actually have a negative impact on an interaction or relationship. "Those shoes look great on you/with your outfit" is more specific. Also, try to direct the compliment at a specific behavior or accomplishment and not the person's character or overall qualities. For example, instead of saying "You are so well-spoken," try "You did a great job on that presentation. I really liked it when you . . ."

Constructive Criticism

Giving negative feedback may be necessary in any relationship. It should, however, be constructive or directed in a way that can help, rather than intended to simply criticize or hurt. It should not be given in the heat of the moment or when you are experiencing strong negative emotions.

You want to be specific when giving constructive criticism. Focus on the problematic behavior you observed, avoid making a judgment about the person, and make an appropriate suggestion. For example, if you go to a restaurant with a friend and they snap rudely at the waiter, constructive feedback might sound like, "Snapping fingers can be interpreted as rude by some waitstaff. You might try making eye contact to get their attention instead."

Determining Your Wants and Needs

If you could have—or have more of—something good in your life, what would that be? What do you need on a personal, professional, or interpersonal level to feel satisfied *right now*? What about a year from now?

Has it been a while since you've asked yourself these questions? Is it hard to answer them?

Knowing what we want and need in our lives is necessary if we are to live life purposefully and feel fulfilled. We need to assert ourselves to get the things we want or need to arrive at that sense of fulfillment. Think about it: You might want a raise at work, or need to feel respected by a friend who always shows up late to meet you. You could wait and see if these changes happen naturally, but wouldn't it be more efficient to ask for or talk about these things, rather than waiting for a change that may never come? People too often feel guilty or selfish for having needs or wants, so they avoid thinking about them at all or put others first. The result is that people ride passively in the passenger seat, living the life they happened upon instead of the one they set out for. This can lead them to feel lost and inauthentic. Also, ignoring their own wants and needs and focusing on the needs of others create imbalanced relationships, making them feel unseen and unsupported by the people around them.

Repeat after me: *I don't need to feel guilty or selfish for wanting or needing things. I am allowed to have things and live life purposefully.*

So, what does this have to do with assertiveness? Once you can identify your wants and needs, you can know when it is important to assert yourself.

Communicating Assertively with Yourself

Assertive self-communication is essential in determining your wants and needs. It also makes you better able to communicate assertively with others. You need to be able to talk honestly and respectfully with yourself to label what you want and need, so you can communicate this confidently to others. Let's work on this together now.

First, let's be clear on the difference between wants and needs. A need refers to something you require to be a physically and psychologically healthy individual. A want is anything else that brings you joy, but isn't required for you be that healthy and complete person.

ACTIVITY: WHAT DO I NEED?

As individuals, we have some common needs.[25] Read the following list of statements and indicate whether each is true for you.

	ITEM	TRUE/FALSE
1.	I feel connected in my relationships with friends, family, and intimate partner.	....
2.	I feel in control of my life and capable of taking steps necessary to make positive changes for myself.	....
3.	My physical needs are met. I have enough food, water, shelter, and am in good health.	....
4.	The people in my life have honesty and integrity.	....
5.	My life has meaning and purpose.	....

If you responded false to statement #1, you may need to feel more connected to others, to feel loved, or to have a stronger sense of belonging, community, or companionship. If statement #2 is false for you, you need autonomy or agency. Responding false to statement #3 indicates a need for meeting more basic physical or biological needs. With statement #4, a false response means you might have a need for honesty. A false response to statement #5 suggests a need to feel that your life has meaning or purpose.

Developing Healthy Boundaries

Boundaries are the invisible limits of what we allow for ourselves in relationships with others, based on our needs and comfort levels. Boundaries can be physical (personal space, time, material possessions, acceptable touching), mental (thoughts and opinions), and emotional (feelings, owning our emotions and not owning others' emotions). Boundaries are essential to our psychological health, self-esteem, self-respect, and personal identity. Setting boundaries is a form of self-care, as healthy boundaries facilitate self-esteem and self-respect by allowing us to maintain our sense of identity. Unhealthy boundaries, on the other hand, result in a weak or unstable sense of identity, where our thoughts, feelings, and actions are inconsistent and dependent on how others think, feel, or act.

Misconceptions about boundaries are plentiful and can prevent people from setting the boundaries they need. One misconception is that it can be too late to set a boundary with someone you already have a relationship with. You *always have the right* to add or adjust your boundaries. For example, if you always say yes when your boss asks you to stay late, it is not too late to start saying no and set a physical boundary that reflects a need for respect of your time. Another misconception about boundaries is that they can prevent intimacy and closeness. This couldn't be further from the truth. Boundaries allow you to build safe and meaningful intimacy with others by allowing your individuality to be seen and respected in the relationship.

Examples of healthy boundaries include the following:

- An employee has a boundary for their personal time with family and won't check work emails at home.

- A woman has a physical boundary for her space and does not allow a partner she is dating to leave belongings at her house or stay over too many nights a week.

- A kid has a physical boundary about touch and tells others he does not want to be tickled or to give hugs.

- An adult son has a mental boundary around his views on politics and won't talk about political matters with his parents, who try to persuade him to think differently.

Setting boundaries isn't a one-time thing; it's an ongoing learning process that requires follow-through. You will learn a lot about yourself, your needs, and what you allow in relationships, and this will influence what boundaries you set or modify. It can feel awkward when first setting and maintaining boundaries, but just like other skills, it will get easier with practice. The general process of boundary setting looks like this:

1. Recognize what your boundaries are *right now*. I emphasize "right now" because boundaries can change. You may not know you have certain boundaries until you find yourself in a situation where you feel uncomfortable. Pay attention to these feelings of discomfort because they will tell you where your boundaries are.

2. Communicate your boundaries to others. This is important because only you know what your boundaries are; others can't read your mind.

3. Protect your boundaries. When someone crosses your boundaries, gently remind them where your limits are. They may have simply forgotten. However, if they continue to cross your boundaries, be firm in your body language and express that this is unacceptable. Some ways of asserting this include:

   - Using an "I statement."
     - "I feel frustrated when you yell at me during a disagreement. Please stop."

   - Clarify why the boundary is there.
     - "For me to feel safe and respected in this relationship, I need you not to yell at me."

   - Firmly restate what you need.
     - "I need you to stop yelling at me."

Dealing with Pushback

Right now, you are working to change the way you communicate. That's awesome! Sometimes when one person initiates change, however, it forces other people in their life to change as well. They may need to change their expectations of you, the way they communicate with you, and/or their behaviors involving you. This can be uncomfortable for them. They may not welcome the change and might push back when you assert yourself or try to set boundaries. They might say no to your requests or try to cross your boundaries. Remember that you decided to initiate this change, make this request, or set these boundaries for a reason. Remind yourself of this intention and why making this change was important for you. Stand up for these reasons and continue to assert yourself firmly. It will get easier in time.

What If I Don't Feel Safe?

If you do not feel safe asserting yourself in a situation or with a specific person, honor this hesitation and wait. It can be genuinely unsafe to be assertive in some situations, like an abusive relationship. Please use your best judgment and reach out to a local therapist or teletherapist to talk about your assertiveness goals in these situations and identify safe ways of meeting your needs. PsychologyToday.com is a great resource to help people find therapists for their specific needs and allows you to filter by many parameters, including health insurance coverage and location.

Now that the basic assertiveness skills have been outlined, practice what you have learned by going through the following exercises. Remember that this is practice. You're not going to be perfect at it, and it might seem a little awkward. That's perfectly okay and normal. Be kind to yourself and engage in this practice without internal negative self-criticism.

EXERCISES

1. Find Your "Power Pose"

Get a sense of how different passive, aggressive, and assertive body language feels by practicing the different nonverbal communication techniques described in the table on page 26. Then, identify your power pose. Describe and maybe even draw what it looks like here.

2. Body Language

In a conversation with someone this week, pay attention to their nonverbal communication. What is their body communicating to you? Is it consistent with what they are telling you verbally?

3. Did You Hear That?

Next time you are in conversation with someone, work on your assertive listening. How did you show them you were listening?

_____

_____

_____

_____

_____

_____

_____

_____

_____

_____

_____

_____

_____

_____

_____

_____

_____

_____

_____

_____

4. Identify Your Wants

Take a few minutes and write what you might want from the following life categories: personal goals/development, relationships, career/schooling, finances, physical/emotional. Now identify one actionable way you can use assertiveness skills to help you get it.

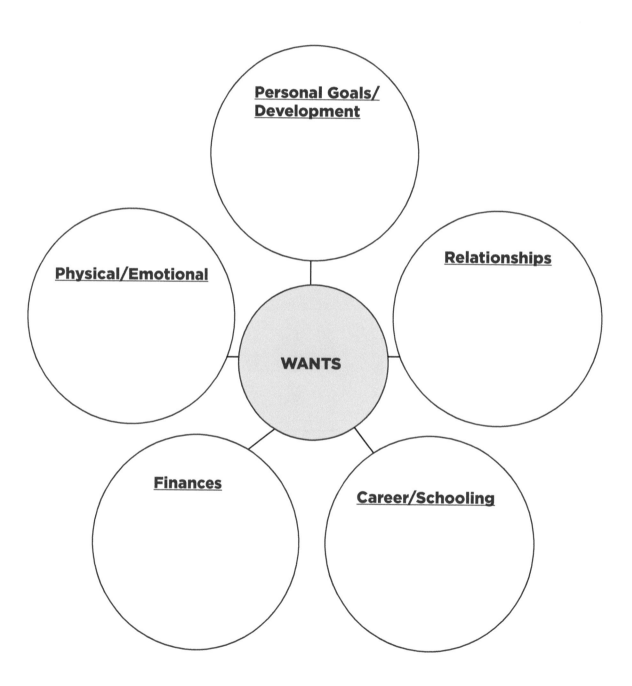

5. Why, Thank You

Try giving someone a compliment. If they respond by giving you a compliment, practice saying "thank you" and accepting the compliment. How did this feel?

_____

_____

_____

_____

_____

_____

_____

6. I Statements

Practice using the "I statement" technique. Think about a time you were hurt by someone's actions. Complete the statement.

I feel _____

_____ when you

_____.

_____.

Please _____

_____.

7. Practice in the Real World

List two *easy* situations where you can practice your assertive communication skills. You should feel safe in these situations and that the stakes are low or could only yield a small impact.

Situation 1: ....

....

....

....

....

Situation 2: ....

....

....

....

....

8. Practice in the Real World, Continued

Practice the situations in exercise 7. Describe your experiences. How do you think you did?

....

....

....

....

....

....

....

....

_____

_____

_____

_____

_____

_____

_____

_____

_____

_____

_____

9. What Boundaries Do I Need Right Now?

Consider the different categories of boundaries and identify a boundary for each that you need now.

Physical: _____

_____

_____

Emotional: _____

_____

_____

Mental: _____

_____

_____

10. Boundary Crossings

Write out an assertive response to these boundary crossings:

1. A friend drops by unannounced and you have other plans.

2. Your partner tells you that you are not allowed to go to a concert without them. You already have tickets to go with a friend.

3. A family member makes negative comments about your weight.

4. Your manager is upset and yells at you in front of your coworkers.

....

....

....

....

....

5. A roommate eats your food and shrugs it off because they forgot to go to the store.

....

....

....

....

....

....

CHAPTER THREE

ASSERTIVENESS AT WORK

Most adults spend half of their waking hours at work.[26] This big commitment of our time makes it important that we feel safe, secure, respected, and valued at work, and that we have positive relationships with our coworkers. These conditions will improve our quality of life, and communicating assertively will help us achieve this.

Assertiveness has also been shown to decrease daily stress and reduce our chances of burnout,[27] which refers to the mental and physical exhaustion, stress, and apathy that can result from overextending ourselves and feeling a loss of personal control in the workplace.[28] The chances are also very high that you will need to assert yourself at some point in your job or career. While many of the basic assertiveness skills discussed previously will still apply, this chapter will focus on special considerations for asserting yourself in the workplace and in your work relationships.

Communication at Work

If you are spending half of your conscious life at work, your work communication is a big part of your total communication and your life. The rules for communication in the workplace might vary by the type of job you do, but communication at work should be professional and have more boundaries overall.

When talking with friends with whom you feel comfortable, there may be only a few (if any) topics you won't discuss or don't feel comfortable discussing. This lack of limits results from the commonalities you typically have with friends, people you deliberately chose to have in your life. This is not necessarily true for coworkers, as you may not share things in common and you usually don't get to choose them. This does not mean that you can't be friends with the people at work, but more limits are needed to protect your and others' sense of identity and values. Whether you enforce these boundaries too loosely, which might suggest a passive communication style, or too strictly, suggesting an aggressive style of communication, could have significant consequences for you.

Some work boundaries may include:

Mental. An additional mental boundary regarding safe and appropriate topics should exist at work. For example, talking about sex with a coworker could make them or you uncomfortable, and thus crosses boundaries of feeling safe. It could also violate your company's sexual harassment policies. Talking about politics or other controversial topics can similarly cross a boundary that violates rights of respect for opinions and beliefs. Being too passive with these boundaries could lead to feelings of negative personal judgment or discomfort. However, enforcing these boundaries too aggressively could make you appear cold and impersonal, because others don't have any idea how you think, what you stand for, or what interests you.

Physical. Physical boundaries at work might reflect a need for more or less personal space when you're near others. If you work in an office, you may need more personal space and feel uncomfortable when people stand too close or crowd your desk. If you work as a healthcare professional, you might find at times you need less personal space so you can get close enough to your patients to examine or treat them. Remember to pay attention to how you feel, as this will help you determine where your boundaries are.

Other physical boundaries at work might relate to your time. Passivity here might look like discomfort in saying no to requests for your time, and this could result in taking on more than you can handle, exhaustion, and resentment. Being too aggressive with your time could look like you're not being a "team player," or you're being stubborn or you're not invested in your work.

Emotional. Emotional boundaries at work include a demarcation between your feelings and self-esteem and the feelings of the people you work with. Being passive in maintaining this boundary might result in you taking others' emotions or reactions personally or sacrificing your needs to make others happy. You might stay late because your boss is in a bad mood and you think this will make them feel better. Maintaining this boundary too rigidly might result in difficulty taking responsibility for your actions or how they affect others, such as slacking on a project, leaving a coworker feeling over-worked, and not caring or taking responsibility for this.

Some common issues that come up with work communication include miscommunication, especially in email or writing, and coming across as insubordinate. These can be indicators that you are communicating too passively or aggressively. For example, when sending emails, you may be aware that your writing can seem too "to the point" or rude so you might include several niceties (e.g., "Hope your day is going well") or not communicate as honestly or directly as needed in a particular situation. If a document is needed by noon one day, you might ask your coworker for feedback and to look at it "if they have a chance," thus not communicating the urgency. Your coworker might interpret this as something that can wait and thus might not look at it before it is due. To avoid this, be direct in your emails. You can certainly include niceties in email communication, but make sure to include the important information. If something is due at a certain time, let it be known and be direct about it.

Another problem with work communication actually includes how a person communicates *about* work to other people like significant others or family members. The way you communicate about work or the people you work with can influence your perception of control at work, and this could in turn shape how you communicate at work. Imagine that you just had a difficult workday when your boss was overbearing and critical. Now, you come home and tell your partner all about the "crazy stuff" your "psycho boss" said to you that day. This type of venting could exaggerate the power differential between you and your boss, reinforce a tolerance for being disrespected by your boss, create a feeling of lack of control in the relationship, and cause you to engage in more passive or passive-aggressive communication with your boss in the future.

Peers and Coworkers

Peers and coworkers can also be a source of support in times of crisis. This doesn't mean you need to be close friends, but being friendly while still assertive is the goal. Assertiveness with coworkers should look respectful and considerate, and it should feel equal.

If you are friends with your coworkers or even dating a coworker, your boundaries might be a little more flexible. You might have different needs for the professional relationship and for the personal relationship. For example, you trust a coworker you are dating with more personal information, but you might have a stricter physical boundary in the workplace and need them to protect your privacy by not sharing intimate details in the office.

If you find yourself feeling uncomfortable or resentful around a coworker, it's probably time to set some boundaries. Review the skill guidelines in the chapter 2 Practice section (page 28). First, identify exactly what is leading to these feelings. Which of your needs is not being met? Next, think of how you want to communicate this need to your coworker and how their behavior conflicts with your needs. Remember that what you say should be respectful and direct, not rude or accusatory.

Next, pick your moment. Find an appropriate time and place to address your coworker. Avoid doing this in front of others, unless you don't feel safe talking to this person alone. It also shouldn't be in the heat of the moment. If either of you are feeling strong negative emotions, this might not be the best time for a respectful conversation. Take a break, calm down, and then come back to it. When you start the conversation, be mindful of using assertive body language and listening. Finally, respond to what your coworker says, and reassert yourself if needed.

Situations that require assertive communication will arise with coworkers. For example, you might have a coworker who makes offensive slurs that make you feel unsafe or make the work environment unfriendly. Maybe you have a coworker who consistently tries to initiate a personal connection that you do not want, calling you during your personal time to hang out or flirting with you at work. You may need or want to address these situations using assertiveness. Here are sample scripts of how you could address a few possible issues.

Sample Script

A coworker makes offensive slurs that make you feel unsafe or that the work environment is unfriendly.

> **YOU:** I feel uncomfortable when you make negative comments about people's sexual orientation.

> **COWORKER:** Why are you uncomfortable? What are you, gay?

> **YOU:** My sexual orientation doesn't matter. These comments are offensive and interfere with my ability to do my job here with you. I'd like you to stop.

Your coworker isn't doing their share of the work and it negatively affects you.

> **YOU:** Let's talk about our work on Project X. It is my understanding that I am responsible for doing Y and you are responsible for doing Z. Am I understanding this correctly?

> **COWORKER:** That sounds about right.

YOU: Okay, great. Can you give me an update on your part?

COWORKER: Oh, I haven't really started my part yet. I'm working on a lot of other projects right now.

YOU: I need Y from you for me to do my part. I'm concerned about us not completing this project on time. Could we come up with a timeline that works for both of us?

A coworker consistently tries to initiate a personal connection with you that you do not want (e.g., calling you during your personal time to hang out or flirting with you at work).

YOU: When you call me at home after hours or ask to meet up on the weekends, I get the impression that you are interested in having a personal relationship outside of work. Am I reading this right?

COWORKER: Yeah, I really like you and think we have a lot in common.

YOU: Thank you for clarifying, but I want to keep our relationship professional.

Here are some assertive phrases that can help you communicate with peers and coworkers:

Helpful Phrases

"I'm not comfortable with this [or talking about this]."

"We're both here to work and I'd like it if we could keep things professional. Specifically, please do not [list the boundary crossing behavior, such as calling after work hours]."

"Let's talk about how we are going to divide the workload."

"I would really appreciate your help with [whatever appropriate need you have, like understanding how the register works]."

Meetings

Much of our discussion on assertive communication has focused on how to assert yourself with another person one-on-one. There may be times, however, when you will need to assert yourself in a more public setting, and it is important to know how you might need to adjust your approach. For example, during a meeting you might be asked to do something that would be redundant, is an ineffective use of your time, or is based on incorrect information. Or maybe your boss is considering promoting you or one of your colleagues to lead a creative project and holds a meeting to assess everyone's project ideas. Speaking up in these situations could save you time and frustration, or give you résumé-building opportunities that you would otherwise miss.

The minute you enter a meeting you should be *on* and mindful of using confident and assertive body language. You also want to pay close attention and listen closely to the person holding the meeting, especially their introduction of its purpose and agenda. Next, you want to read the room. Who is the audience and what is the emotional tone? If your goal in the meeting is to assert yourself by expressing an idea, make sure it ties back to the overall purpose of the meeting, is germane to the context of the meeting, and is appropriate for the emotional tone and audience of the room. Then, make your own opportunity to speak and advocate for yourself and your ideas; this shows confidence. Don't wait for someone to invite you to speak. Also, if you aren't jumping in to speak, people might assume that you don't have any ideas worth sharing. This doesn't mean that you should interrupt while others are talking, though; instead, take advantage of pauses in conversation. If you find yourself in a situation where a colleague is dominating the discussion and leaving no pause to jump into, try making your intention to speak known with a phrase like "I have an idea I'd like to discuss."

You might need to assert yourself in a meeting in a different way. For example, what if a coworker tries to hand off a time-consuming project to you that you realistically don't have the time to devote to? People who have a more aggressive communication style might utilize a public setting to make unreasonable requests, counting on a person to say yes out of feeling pressured by the social setting. In these instances, one strategy you could use is to ask for time to think about the request. This gives you time to collect your thoughts, think about what you want to say, and pick a more comfortable moment to address the person again.

Sample Script

COWORKER: I think you would really enjoy a project I'm working on right now, and your background might actually be a better fit for it. How would you like to take it on?

YOU: Thank you for thinking of me for this project. Unfortunately, I don't have the time to take on any new projects.

COWORKER: Are you sure? I think you would really like it.

YOU: I'm sure. I probably would like it, but I just don't have the time.

"I'll have to think about this. Can I let you know in an hour/by the end of the day?"

"I have an idea I'd like to discuss."

"I'd rather not use this meeting time to discuss that. Can we discuss this after the meeting?"

Dealing with Technology

Technology has changed workplace communication markedly from previous generations. Beyond the older communication methods of telephone, email, and sticky notes, we have video chat and social media platforms that allow people to be in constant communication.

There are definite advantages to this. People and organizations can exchange ideas faster and more broadly and answer questions faster. In hospitals and medical facilities this could literally save lives. In addition to speed and efficiency, today's workplace communication benefits workers by allowing them more freedom to work remotely, although this depends on job type. Remote working means employees can log into work, talk to employees, broker deals, or perform other job tasks from anywhere they have an internet or a phone connection. You could work anytime and anywhere!

Wait a second. *You could work anytime and anywhere?!*

Technology can quickly become disadvantageous to your personal life. The line between personal time and work time can be faint or hard to distinguish, resulting in your boundaries potentially being crossed more easily or more frequently. Technology and "tele-pressure" can also influence our expectations or beliefs about what makes us good workers, potentially creating anxiety. For example, if your workplace praises the employee who is always on call or reachable, you might believe that you aren't as good or committed, or you are putting your job in jeopardy if you ignore calls during your personal time. These beliefs can lead to employees anxiously checking emails, logging in or answering "quick calls" on vacation, all of which can eat up their personal time or take them away from time with loved ones. This can contribute to burnout, anxiety, and negative self-perception. This section will address how to effectively assert yourself across technology platforms, including phone, email, and video-conferencing.

Phone

If you are new to asserting yourself or if you experience social anxiety, you might find it easier to start practicing your skills over the phone. Not seeing the other person's face and their reaction to what you say might take the pressure off, especially if you need to make a difficult request. Additionally, if you struggle with assertive body language, phone communication could feel easier by allowing you to focus on your words and how you say them—the context surrounding what you say and tone of voice—rather than all of this *and* your body language.

There are several ways in which you might need to assert yourself over the phone in your work. The first involves protecting your time. If you are off the clock or homesick with your phone on mute and you get a call from work, how would you maintain your boundary? This may depend on the type of job you have and your employer's specific policies regarding reachability. If neither your job type nor company policies dictates that you are required to be available by phone on your personal time, and yet you still receive calls from colleagues after hours for non-urgent matters, you may need to state with a firm voice that you are unavailable and indicate when you will be.

Participating in a conference call also requires assertiveness skills. How do you join in the conversation without coming across as rude? Do your colleagues typically just jump in, or do they announce that they want to speak? Pay attention to your company conference call culture and try to practice their standard. You may also practice assertiveness by asking what the call norm is the first time you speak, with a statement like "Is this how we typically take our turn?"

If it doesn't seem like your workplace has any standard way of interjecting, try experimenting with different methods and see how you feel about the outcome. In terms of addressing a coworker who is talking over you on the phone, consider the context and why they are interrupting you. Did you misspeak or provide incorrect information and they are correcting you? If so, it might be appropriate for them to interrupt you. Or, maybe they are leaving the call early and need to share their information before hanging up. If their interruption does not seem to have a logical reason, then address the coworker in a kind but firm matter. If the coworker ignores this and continues, then you may need to weigh the pros and cons of letting them speak first. You might find that having a disagreement over the phone in the presence of others is more disrupting or harmful than talking next. After the call is complete, if you have the means of talking to the coworker in person, or at least on a one-on-one call, you can talk to the coworker then.

When starting a new job, you may be asked to do a phone interview prior to an in-person interview. You may need to advocate for yourself when discussing compensation, your qualifications, or your past experiences. Using assertive body language is also important in this context. I know, you're on the phone and they can't see you, but it's possible that some nonverbal cues and communication can be transmitted over the phone. This means that you should dress the part, sit down in a chair with good posture instead of sitting on your bed or slouching, and smile. Remember the power pose from chapter 2 (see page 24)? These nonverbal displays can positively influence your confidence and help put you in the professional headspace you need to do well.

Email

Email correspondence might be the most frequently used form of communication in most workplaces, other than talking with coworkers in person. Emails can be sent quickly from your phone or computer, wherever you are. They can save time by allowing direct communication about important topics without all the social back-and-forth and small talk common during in-person conversations. Email messages can be easily misinterpreted, however, and this can contribute to conflict among coworkers.

Follow a couple of key guidelines when you need to assert yourself via email. First, try to avoid lengthy emails. Aim to be direct in your message, using as few words as possible. Second, find an appropriate balance of pleasantries. If you email the same coworkers every day, it's not necessary to include detailed greetings and sign-offs each time. They should also be consistent with the tone of your email. If you are emailing a coworker to address a problem, deliver constructive criticism, or make a request, it might seem contradictory to include a lot of pleasantries. When you do include pleasantries, make sure they are sincere and don't overdo them. If you are making a request of someone or asking for a favor, but still want to include some social sentiments, then place them at the end of your email. Placing these niceties before an ask might come across as insincere or as an attempt to butter up a person to agree to your request. Third, be direct and include important information, such as deadlines or other timeline information, observations or facts about disputes or concerns, and clear divisions of responsibilities about shared projects. Finally, consider how your emails can help you maintain your work-life boundaries. For example, setting an auto-reply message when you are out of office can help set the expectation that you are unavailable then and will not be checking emails. Setting this boundary might result in people emailing you less after hours.

Video-conferencing

Video-conferencing can be a powerful communication tool. The ability to see others' facial reactions provides emotional context that might result in more accurate communication. Be mindful of your body language when video-conferencing. Try to keep your focus on the image on your screen and avoid extraneous glances to your surroundings, which might come across as distraction or lack of interest. Make sure you are speaking up so others can hear you. If you are on a call with people who might not recognize you, such as colleagues who work out of state or in a different country, be sure to introduce yourself when you speak.

Pay attention to your surroundings and set up your camera to reveal only what you want your audience to see. This is one way you can protect your privacy boundaries. Are you comfortable with others seeing your family photos or personal mementos behind you? Additionally, try to keep outside noises to a minimum, such as the TV, noisy pets, or screaming children in the background. This last one can be hard! If you are conferencing in from a location that is going to be noisy, take care to keep your microphone muted when you are not speaking.

Here is a sample script for addressing a coworker assertively, along with some helpful phrases to use with peers and coworkers.

Sample Script

Imagine that you're in the middle of talking on a conference call and your coworker, Todd, talks over you to take the conversation in a different direction.

YOU: Todd, I'd really love to hear your thoughts on that topic. Please let me finish my thoughts first.

COWORKER: [Ignores you, continues to talk over you.]

YOU: It seems we are both talking at the same time. I'd like to wrap up what I was saying before you shift the conversation to a new topic.

Helpful Phrases

"I'd love to hear more about your thoughts on this. Please let me finish my thoughts first and then we can discuss your ideas."

"I'm unavailable today, but I can talk with you more about this when I return to work on _____ day."

Management

Being a manager can be a mixed bag! It may be one of the most fulfilling roles you will ever have, but it can also be incredibly challenging. Many managers did not choose the role, but assumed it after a certain amount of tenure or after a promotion. Excelling as an individual worker doesn't necessarily prepare a person to manage the workload of other people, or delegate to each of them in a way that meets the company's goals as well as their own. These skills take years to develop, and, if you're like most managers, instead of receiving training and time to practice, you were pushed in front of your new team and told to go for it.

Being a Manager

As a manager, it can be easy to accidentally cross an employee's boundaries. Involved in more senior-level conversations, you are acutely aware of the needs of the business, likely more than any of your employees. You can quickly forget the individual needs of your employees by focusing on the needs of the company and trying to push your team to be as productive as possible. Further, your employees may be willing to let you cross those boundaries if they are not used to asserting themselves, due to the power differential between you. Assertive listening and paying attention to nonverbal communication can be an integral way of learning what your employees are trying to express.

On the flip side, it may feel like employees are sometimes trying to take advantage of you. They may push deadlines or miss shifts, and always have a reason for their behavior when pressed: "My car broke down," "My grandma passed away," or "I've been really sick." Where do you draw the line between understanding and accommodating the needs of your employee and saying that enough is enough? This can be an incredibly difficult conversation to have, and one where your assertiveness skills will be essential. The guidelines for setting boundaries discussed in chapter 2 (see page 33) still apply, along with these additional points to consider.

1. If the boundary you are trying to set relates to employees crossing your boundary, ask yourself if the boundary violation is occurring with just one employee or most of them. If it is just with one, address them assertively one-on-one. If most of your employees are crossing the boundary, then it might be best to set a meeting to address the whole team.

2. Model appropriate boundaries. Even if you are working after hours, don't assume others are or want to be. Try not to send work emails to employees after hours, and, if you need to, express that it is appropriate for them to respond when they are next working. If you draft emails at night, your email platform may have an option for scheduling emails to be sent later, during business hours.

Don't discuss your personal life with employees. While it is acceptable for them to know general things about your personal life—if you are married, have kids, or any specific hobbies—you shouldn't disclose intimate details, and you should definitely not solicit their advice or use them as a therapist.

3. Encourage discussions with your employees about professional boundaries.

4. Consider your workplace's culture, mission statement, and policies to help you sharpen your ideas about what boundaries, and consequences for crossing them, are appropriate for your company.

5. Express clear expectations for employee behavior and work. This doesn't mean you need to micromanage. It pays to be flexible and allow employees to try out what works for them whenever possible, but sometimes there will be nonnegotiable boundaries that need to be expressed.

Sample Script

YOUR EMPLOYEE: Sorry, I wasn't able to work on the report this week. My car broke down and it's been a nightmare to fix.

YOU AS A MANAGER: I'm sorry to hear about your car; that sounds stressful. In situations like this where you are not sure you can get a report completed by the deadline, please give me as much notice as you can. Then I can determine if it needs to be reassigned or evaluate other options for getting it done. This report does have a hard deadline of Friday. Do you think you will have enough time to complete it by then?

YOUR EMPLOYEE: Geez, I don't know.

YOU AS A MANAGER: What would you need to get this done?

YOUR EMPLOYEE: I would need to stop working on my other projects, too.

YOU AS A MANAGER: Okay. I can get a colleague to cover your other projects until after this report is completed.

Being Managed

Asserting yourself to your manager can be daunting. This person has direct authority over you and your livelihood, and a common fear is that assertiveness will be misconstrued as insubordination and lead to negative career consequences. However, recall the differences between assertiveness and other communication styles from chapter 1, like aggressiveness or passive aggression (see page 2). By maintaining an appropriate tone, positive body language, and a clear, appropriate expression of your needs, you can avoid sounding like a chronic complainer and move toward getting your work needs met. Consider these additional notes about setting boundaries with your manager.

1. Clarify expectations. Make sure you and your manager agree on expectations for work, personal time, etc. Identify whether your manager may have unrealistic expectations and address them using facts instead of emotion. For example, "While I am on vacation with my family, I expect to be unavailable by phone or email" rather than "I feel bad that I won't be able to help the team while I'm away."

2. If you find yourself needing to say no to your manager, offer a concrete reason and an alternative solution if possible. For example, "With my current workload, I am unable to do X. If the deadline is flexible, I could do it at a later time. If it's a hard deadline, it might be best assigned to a colleague who has more time right now."

3. Ask for what you need in order to succeed in your job or have a work-life balance that works for you. Be willing to problem-solve with your manager to get your needs met.

4. Don't take your manager's emotions or reactions personally. They reflect only on them and their ability to regulate their emotions, not on you.

5. A note about gender. Research indicates that even when expressing assertiveness in the workplace in identical ways, men and women may experience different outcomes. Findings suggest that assertiveness from women is inconsistent with expectations for female gender norms. A woman using the same

assertiveness strategies as a man might result in her appearing competent but also less likable, "bitchy," or other negative attributes.[30] Is this fair? Absolutely not! So, what do you do if you're a woman, or even non-binary but perceived as a woman, and want to negotiate a raise or make requests, such as extra time to work on a project?

Research suggests that women who are successful in advocating for themselves in the workplace use "strategic assertiveness," or adjusting their assertive approach to match the social context. This approach is similar to *reading the room* and *knowing your audience*. Interestingly, this research demonstrates that women who advocate beyond themselves—for the team they work on or manage, for instance—are just as successful as men using the same strategies. Framing self-advocacy as advocacy for others as well is a potential strategy to improve assertiveness effectiveness. So, instead of asking for a raise for yourself, try framing it as benefiting your family, work team, or community. Another strategy is to ask a colleague or additional supervisor to advocate on your behalf.[29, 30] Again, it's not fair that women need to do this, but strategies like this may help get you what you need and even narrow the wage gap disparity between men and women.

Aside from the issues caused by the power differential between yourself and your manager, let's examine other common problems that can make the relationship with your manager tricky to navigate.

Even though we're not supposed to, we all often end up choosing favorites. Unfortunately, managers are no different. Research suggests that managers create ingroups and outgroups, giving favored projects or opportunities to employees in their ingroup, and giving less enjoyable or beneficial projects to those in the outgroup.[31] This can damage the growth and development of anyone stuck in the outgroup who wants to advance in their career. If you find yourself in a situation like this, assertiveness can help you address your concerns with your manager and advocate for yourself to get the professional opportunities you need.

For some others, the issue isn't a manager who doesn't care enough, but one who doesn't care at all. We call this the *laissez-faire* management style: being hands-off and letting employees make their own decisions. This type of manager won't help you when problems arise or identify development opportunities. You will need to assert yourself to make your desires known and work on getting them met. This can be particularly challenging as your manager may be so set in their style that it is difficult for them to meet your needs. If this is the case, you can talk to your manager about reaching out to others to get your needs met. Though this sounds like it could be an awkward conversation, it's not! In fact, many jobs have this type of relationship readily available to employees in the form of a mentor or sponsor. Letting your manager know that you would like a mentor should not be seen as problematic, but instead as a positive sign of your desire to grow and advance your skills. What manager doesn't want their employees to do that?

Even if your manager isn't hands-off, there will be times that you'll need to manage up, or manage your manager, to get your needs met. Nobody knows what you need more than you!

Helpful Phrases

"I'd like to talk to you about something that will help me in my role here at Company X. Can we set up a time to talk about this?"

"I would love the opportunity to take on X. Could we discuss the possibilities for this?"

"I've had a problem with X, but I am working on resolving this through Y."

"I'm concerned about how our team handled project X and would like to discuss this with you."

Customers

If you work with customers, I don't have to tell you how challenging that can be. Having experience working with customers can teach you some invaluable lessons like patience, the importance of saving face, and persistent respect for even the most challenging people. It might seem silly to set boundaries with people you may only interact with once or twice, but trust me when I say it's not. Each customer contributes to your general sense of enjoyment and safety at your job, and that's certainly not silly. The lack of sustained interaction that customers have with you might make them more likely to cross boundaries, because there is less accountability. They might ask you for things that you can't give them, and they may know this. They might demand service on their time, in their way, or in a way that violates your company's policies. They may feel that their "purchasing power" gives them dominion over you, but it doesn't. You have the right to feel respected at your place of work.

When you are providing a service or selling something, particularly when it's your own business or product, you are in a unique position of taking customers' reactions personally or equating whether you make customers happy with your success or helpfulness. This might threaten to stop you from asserting your boundaries, but don't let it. Be honest, work hard, and treat others with the same respect you want in return. Even if you do all these things, though, customers still might not be satisfied, and you will need to assert yourself. Keep the following in mind when you do.

1. Try to step into the customers' shoes and understand their perspective. Is their behavior reasonable based on their context or culture? Even if you can't meet their needs or expectations, consider how you might speak to their context or perspective. For example, you might consider a customer rude for not tipping you. Keep in mind that, in some cultures, it is not customary to tip, so this might not be a slight to you or a sign of rudeness.

2. Be consistent. If you say no, don't waffle on it. Knowing your company's policies and trusting they are there for a reason can help you draw the line regarding what you can and can't do.

3. Know your worth, respect yourself, and pick your battles. What you do is valuable. Customers wouldn't be coming to you soliciting your services if it wasn't. If someone is rude to you and you are only going to interact with them briefly, weigh the cost of letting it go. If your interaction is more prolonged and you don't think you can ignore it, make a firm statement to let them know that their behavior is not acceptable, or consider getting a manager involved.

Sample Script

CUSTOMER: [Asks for a discount that you can't give.]

YOU: Unfortunately, I am not able to discount this service.

CUSTOMER: What?! Come on. It's not like it's your loss.

YOU: It may not be my personal loss, but I cannot discount this service. Is there something else I can help you with?

Helpful Phrases

"I'd love to help you, but I'm not able to give you this specifically. Is there something else I can help you with?"

"I understand that you want X, but unfortunately that is not available."

Now that we've covered why assertiveness is important in the workplace and how to assert yourself with various people you might interact with at work, practice your skills by completing the following exercises. Additionally, look out for opportunities to practice these skills in your current workplace. Remember to start small.

EXERCISES

1. What Work Works for You?

Imagine your ideal day at your job (or a future job if you aren't working now). This is a day where you feel prepared, able, and accomplished. What does it look like? Now, imagine leaving work and knowing that you don't have to think about work until the next day. Maybe you meet up with friends. Maybe you go home and cook yourself a nice meal, exercise, or engage in other activities that feel good to you. Create contrasting lists of features of your ideal working day versus your typical working day. Next, cross out the things you don't like about your actual working days and circle the things that are closer to your ideal.

IDEAL WORKDAY	TYPICAL WORKDAY

2. What Keeps You from Your Ideal Day?

Consider the previous exercise and the items you crossed out in your list of features of your typical day. Why are these features of your current workday? Identify where these features originated. Were they imposed upon you? Did you initiate them?

....

....

....

....

....

....

3. Boundaries at Work

Now consider what mental, physical, and emotional needs you have in the workplace. These are your boundaries for your workplace.

PHYSICAL	EMOTIONAL	MENTAL

4. F-R-I-E-N-D-S

Are you (or have you ever been) friends with any of your coworkers? What issues have come up? Are there any issues you are afraid will arise? Identify them, then describe how assertiveness could be used to address a specific issue.

....

....

....

....

....

....

....

....

....

5. Boundary Contingency Plans: Coworkers

Write an assertive response to each of the following scenarios:

If my coworker is rude, I will ....

....

....

If I'm in a meeting, and it is clear that a coworker is taking my project idea and passing it off as their own, I will ....

....

....

If a coworker continuously asks for my help and it interferes with my time, I will

....

....

....

....

6. Boundary Contingency Plans: Managers

Write an assertive response to each of the following scenarios:

If my manager denies my request for vacation time, I will ....

....

....

If my boss calls after hours, I will ....

....

....

If my boss asks me to do a project I don't feel qualified for, I will ....

....

....

7. Unexpected Feedback

Your manager calls you into their office to say that a colleague feels you are not "pulling your weight" and are hard to reach by phone or email, usually after hours. This feedback catches you completely off guard. What do you say to your manager?

....

....

....

....

....

8. Body Language

How might your body language look different when talking to your manager (or teacher or peer, if you don't have a manager), compared to talking to a friend?

....

....

....

....

....

9. Aggressive Communication: Okay or Not Okay?

Do you think there are any situations when it might be appropriate to display more aggressive body language (e.g., raised voice, arms folded, sarcastic tone, etc.) with a coworker? What about with a manager? Justify your answer.

10. So, How Am I Doing?

Imagine that you are a new employee at a company. You are currently being managed by someone who lacks essential managerial skills. They constantly complain about their wife to you and your colleagues. They often forget to write out a schedule for their employees and typically let you know when you are needed to work the day before a shift. They also expect you to stay late to do extra work "off the clock." Now, they have called you in to get feedback about their management style. What do you say?

11. Let It Go

List two situations in which you may choose not to assert yourself.

1. ....

2. ....

12. Can You Hear My Smile?

Call up a friend or family member and practice smiling during your initial greeting. Next, try calling someone else and giving the same initial greeting, but this time, don't smile. Maybe even frown a little. Ask each person if they could tell whether you were smiling or not. Then, ask yourself if you felt different on either call, or if the person you greeted might have responded in accordance with your facial expression.

....

....

....

....

....

....

....

....

....

13. Caught on Camera . . .

If you were working from home and had to video-conference into work, what would your setup be? What might you be revealing to your colleagues?

....

....

....

....

14. Manage Up!

If you are currently working and being managed, consider what you might need from you manager to help you do your best work (e.g., training in a specific area, a mentor, more opportunities to take on projects consistent with your interests or background, etc.). How could you manage up and advocate for these things with your manager? Come up with an assertive phrase that you could use.

....

....

....

....

15. 1 Star! Worst Service/Product Ever!

Imagine that you are a business owner and you receive a 1-star review from a customer. You are able to write a reply to their comment. How would you respond assertively to them?

....

....

....

....

CHAPTER FOUR
ASSERTIVENESS AT HOME

Family. This word can make you cringe or smile. It could refer to those who brought you into this world, the ones you learned alongside and fought with growing up, or the family you created yourself, either through biology or by choice. Our familial relationships can be the simplest, most intimate, and longest-running in our lives. Despite this closeness and longevity, they are often replete with conflict and poor boundaries. Sometimes it's the people closest to us, those who know us the best, who can hurt us the most deeply. This is why it is important to be able to assert yourself in these relationships. This chapter will discuss the special considerations of being assertive with family.

Family

Asserting yourself with parents, siblings, and even your own children is challenging for many reasons. Chief among these challenges is the domino effect. As chapter 1 indicated, many of our assertiveness skills are learned from models. If your parents did not model appropriate ways to be assertive, how would you know how to assert yourself with them? Do you even know that you can assert yourself with them? "I didn't know I could say that to them" is a reaction many of my clients have when we begin to work on establishing boundaries with parents.

If your parents didn't teach you assertiveness, chances are they didn't teach this to your siblings, either. Now there is a group of you having potential conflicts and lacking the skills to set boundaries and fight fair. Without intervention, you may adopt passive or aggressive communication styles with your own children, thereby not modeling assertiveness to them and perpetuating the whole cycle again. Let the cycle stop with you.

Parents

When we're young, our parents' words are gospel and law. We typically see our parent or parents as infallible and believe them no matter what. As we grow older and begin questioning the world, however, we begin to doubt that our parents always know what's best. I'm not just talking about being a rebellious teenager here; the way we perceive the world changes as we age, and sometimes the way we see it is different from how our parent or parents view it. This can be the start of serious conflict between yourself and your parents.

Setting boundaries with your parents will be the most difficult thing some of you have ever had to do. This is due not only to personal factors, but values, cultural/societal norms, and your parents' reactions. If you are someone to whom being assertive does not come naturally, this is likely not the first relationship where you want to practice these skills. As mentioned previously in this workbook, do the exercises in this book and then begin practicing in easier situations or with a trusted friend—either in person or over the phone—to hone your skills before tackling a relationship like this.

For others, deference to parents and elders in general is taught and practiced by the society they live in, so the idea of denying a request from a parent or setting personal boundaries that may interfere with their desires is difficult to consider, let alone attempt. Additionally, your parents' response to your attempts at asserting yourself can either encourage you to continue or discourage you so much that you want to run away, screaming, "I'm sorry! I'm sorry!" and never cross them again. If your parents are like mine, they've mastered the art of the guilt trip, a skill they've been using on you *literally* your whole life, and they will use it to try to shut down any idea you have of setting healthy boundaries with them.

Due to how deeply ingrained your relationship is with your parents, there are some specific challenges you can face when trying to assert yourself to them. The first is getting over the sense of betrayal. Your parents have given you everything. They've given you your very life! And now you want to be ungrateful and set boundaries with them? I know, it can be hard to consider, but healthy boundaries are key to maintaining a strong relationship with your parents. Wanting to have your needs met and to feel respected is not betraying your parents or being ungrateful; instead, it is fully valuing your own life as much as you value theirs and asking that they do the same.

Another key challenge you may face when trying to assert yourself with your parents is that you may still live with them. Living away from your parents at least affords you the safety net of not having to rely on them anymore if things go awry! But if you are still in the same home or are financially dependent on your parents, assertiveness can seem much more difficult, and may be met with far more pushback from them. Finally, there could be dependency issues. Maybe your parents have the expectation that you will help support them financially due to cultural norms or personal needs, or they are elderly and depend on you to care for them, overseeing their health, finances, and end-of-life wishes.

Even if your parents are elderly or ill, it is still important to be assertive and express your needs. In fact, this can be particularly true when you have elderly parents. You are now also older, likely with an established life, job, and maybe even a family of your own. Your parents' expectation that you will still do everything they want—just as you did when you were a child—is just not feasible and can have real ramifications for your job, finances, or family.

In summary, setting boundaries with your parents can be *hard*. In this relationship, perhaps more than any other, it is important to remain firm when you are setting your boundaries. Here are some tips for going about this.

1. You should remain calm and avoid using overly emotional language or getting upset. You should repeat your needs and desires, doing your best not to waver.

2. Remain consistent in expressing your needs to demonstrate your seriousness and your resolve. This will help you get what you need from your parents.

3. Based on what you know about your parents, ask yourself what they might need to feel respected—an apology, validation, explanation, etc.—and then ask yourself if you can give this to them while still respecting yourself and meeting your needs. This is an additional step that can help preserve the relationship.

Next, here are two sample scripts for when you express your needs and your parents refuse to honor them. The first applies if you live separately from your parents; the second is how the conversation may go if you still live with your parents and deal with that added barrier to expressing your needs as an individual.

Sample Script #1

Imagine this scenario. You are a grown adult, live two hours away from your parents, work full time and have a family and/or community of your own. Due to work trips, this is the first Saturday you have had to be with your family in a month. Your parents call and ask you to come over to mow their lawn.

YOU: I can't do that this Saturday.

YOUR PARENTS: You know, you haven't been by in a while and the grass is getting long. Your father and I wanted to invite some friends over next week, but not with the yard looking like this!

YOU: I know I haven't been by. I've had to make a lot of work trips this month. Still, I need to be home this Saturday and spend time with my family. I can either come by next week, or you could see if your neighbors' son would be willing to cut the grass.

Sample Script #2

Now, imagine living at home with your parents and they make the same request of you to mow their lawn. Except now, you need to spend the day studying for a final exam on Monday. Sure, maybe you should have started studying earlier, but you rationalize that you couldn't because you have been working a lot of extra shifts.

YOU: Because I have been working extra shifts this week, I've fallen behind on studying. I was planning on using Saturday to study for an exam on Monday. Would you mind if I mowed it after my exam?

YOUR PARENTS: I guess I can get your father to do it, but I didn't want to ask him because of his back problems. *[Yup, that's passive-aggressive!]*

YOU: I don't want you to ask Dad. I will do it after my exam. If I finish studying on Saturday early, I will do it then; otherwise, I will do it after class on Monday.

Helpful Phrases

"I feel strongly about this. You've raised me to think through my choices and that is what I have done. Please respect my opinion."

"I love and respect you. Please respect me."

"I'm happy to discuss my thought process on this, but please do not try to change my mind."

"I am your son/daughter/child, but I am also my own person and I have an obligation to myself to advocate for what I need."

Siblings

I often wonder what it would have been like to be an only child. Don't get me wrong, siblings can be wonderful. I have nine of them, and while they definitely whetted my interest in psychology at a young age, there is no shortage of conflict or frustration. An older sibling might try to exert dominance over you or appoint themselves the decision maker over family matters. A younger sibling might defer to you, leaving you feeling responsible for making decisions.

These actions can create a perception of differences in power, leading to unrealistic or unhealthy expectations. And as you get older and take care of elderly parents, these power differentials can have a big impact on your time, money, emotions, and personal life. If one sibling is forced to be the sole caregiver, it will come at a cost to them. Even if they have the financial resources to do it or willingly agree, they could still find themselves feeling overwhelmed and mentally exhausted, or they may build resentment toward siblings who don't help, which could have lasting effects on the sibling relationships.

Aside from the challenges siblings face regarding responsibility, they can also encounter difficulties related to establishing their own identity outside of the family or sibling relationship. This is particularly true of *enmeshed families*, or families that have poor or diffuse boundaries. This can look like the older sibling who always helps a younger sibling at an expense to themselves or out of a feeling of obligation. It can look like feelings of guilt in response to wanting to make choices for yourself, because you know your sibling or parent will disapprove or that it won't benefit them (e.g., going to school or taking a job across the country).

If you struggle with boundary issues in your sibling relationships in general, you might feel any of the following: a lack of privacy, an overwhelming sense of obligation to your sibling, difficulty separating your emotions or thoughts from theirs, a sense of dependency in the relationship, a sense of responsibility in a sibling's choices, difficulty pursuing your own goals and interests, or low self-esteem related to years of internalized criticism. These aren't good feelings, and setting healthy boundaries is the way to address them.

Boundary setting with siblings, as with parents, can take time and finesse, since these relationships carry years of precedent. Year in and year out, you have reinforced and maintained your communication patterns. You might meet significant resistance for suddenly saying no or refusing to help in the ways you have for years.

One path toward setting boundaries is to start small and build from there. This path is obviously going to be slow, but it could give you and your siblings time to adjust to the changing dynamics. Another more direct path involves sitting your siblings down and having a conversation about your desire to set more boundaries in this and other relationships in your life. Use "I statements." Tell them why you need these boundaries and what changes you hope to see.

Your siblings ultimately care about you and want good things for you. They may not realize how the existing communication patterns negatively affect you, or maybe they do but they don't know another way forward. Also, keep in mind that you may need to have these conversations more than once. Asking someone to change a behavior that they've practiced for years will take time.

Here is a sample script of how you might initiate the second path (having a direct conversation about boundaries) with a sibling.

Sample Script

YOU: I have been feeling exhausted and overextended lately. It's made me think about my needs and the changes I need to make to help me meet them. Specifically, I need to devote more time to my family and for myself after work. This means I won't be able to talk with you on the phone every night anymore.

SIBLING: But you're the only person who gets me! What about my own need for someone to talk through my problems with?

An additional challenging scenario for parents practicing assertiveness is a child's toxic friendship. Parents may want to insist that the child can't spend time with a friend, or find passive ways of interjecting, like delaying or canceling play dates, scheduling other activities, etc. This could make a child feel angry, motivate retaliation, and most importantly limit their ability to think about their friend choices. Engaging your child in a conversation about why they like this friend—which tells you why your child is motivated to keep this friend—and your concerns—which can teach them lessons in boundaries or other important social skills—may be more useful.

Adopting an assertive parenting style is a continual process that requires you to be flexible and adaptive. Your approach will need to change, depending on your child's age, developmental stage, and any psychological or cognitive challenges they may be experiencing. For example, with a younger child you will need to talk in simpler terms or demonstrate appropriate behaviors through more modeling or hand-over-hand techniques instead of using more involved verbal instructions.

In addition to the basic guidelines for demonstrating assertiveness described elsewhere in this book, consider the following tips for developing an assertive parenting approach.

1. Listen to what your child is communicating to you. Children, even those who are young or lack verbal skills, communicate how they are feeling and what they need. Show them that you are listening by reflecting back what they are communicating. For example, "It looks like you're feeling sad because you can't watch your favorite show right now. Is that right?"

2. Involve your child in a conversation. Ask them how they feel or what they think about a particular situation.

3. Be clear about the boundaries you are setting, and briefly state why you are setting these limits.

4. When appropriate, give your child choices to reinforce their autonomy. For young children, this can be a simple choice like "Do you want yogurt or eggs for breakfast?"

5. Remember that you might be your child's most influential model and teacher. Demonstrate appropriate behavior, emotion regulation, empathy, and boundaries. Be sure to offer them praise for demonstrating similar behaviors. This will help reinforce these behaviors.

6. When disciplining to correct behavioral issues, tell them why their behavior was not appropriate, and use a suitable consequence, such as apologizing to someone they hurt or cleaning up a mess they made. Practice unconditional love even when disciplining. Keep the child's actions distinct from who they are. Be careful not to communicate conditions of worth or love, or express that they are only worthy or lovable if they do certain things or behave in certain ways.

If your child has another parent who is involved in child-rearing, then you should discuss and coordinate your parenting approach to facilitate consistency. It can be counterproductive for one parent to adopt an assertive style while the other remains passive or aggressive. Work in tandem with your co-parent as much as possible. If you and your co-parent have a difficult relationship, you might find it helpful to talk with a licensed marriage and family therapist about your parenting approaches.

Sample Script

You just got a call from your child's teacher, reporting that they threw an eraser at another kid and it hit them in the eye. The other child is okay, but the teacher has informed you that she is requiring your child to apologize to the other kid tomorrow, and that your child will miss out on recess for today. After school lets out, you bring up this issue with your child.

YOU: I talked to your teacher about what happened at school today. I'd like us to talk about it. Can you tell me what happened?

YOUNG CHILD: I got an answer wrong and the other kid was being mean and calling me names. I just got so mad and I threw my eraser at him.

YOU: Thank you for telling me. That must have been frustrating. Is there another way that you could have expressed your frustration that wouldn't have led to someone else getting hurt?

YOUNG CHILD: I don't know.

YOU: Okay, well let's come up with some ideas together. Now that this has happened, there will be consequences. Your teacher told me that you had to sit out of recess today. You also need to apologize to your classmate.

Then begin problem-solving and working through an apology, writing it out if age appropriate or using role-play to act it out.

Helpful Phrases

"You are allowed to cry and be upset. If you need help feeling better, I'm here."

"Can you tell me why you are frustrated?"

"Let's see if we can come up with some solutions together."

"It's not okay that you did this. What is another way you can express yourself?"

Hopefully, you now have some more insight into your family and how you can express assertive communication in these relationships. Go through the following exercises to practice. And, as always, be on the lookout for opportunities in real life to practice the techniques and skills you've learned.

EXERCISES

1. Draw It Out

Draw a picture (stick figures count!) of you and your family doing a typical activity. Add thought or word bubbles to each person.

2. I Spy . . .

Review the picture you drew of your family. What family dynamics—relationship or communication patterns, emotions, and boundaries (or lack thereof)—did you communicate in your drawing?

3. Baseline

Rate your level of difficulty asserting yourself to your parents, siblings, children, or other family members on a 1 (no problem asserting myself) to 10 (cannot assert myself) scale. Justify this level by describing why it is difficult for you to assert yourself in this relationship.

RELATIONSHIP	RATING	FACTORS
Parents		
Siblings		
Children		
Other		

4. Not at the Dinner Table

What are some topics you would not want to discuss at the dinner table with family? What topics would cause uproar, criticism, or arguments?

....

....

....

....

....

5. Stop Right There!

Consider and list the boundaries you need from your parents right now. How are these boundaries different now than when you were younger? If you are also a parent, describe your boundaries with your children. Are these boundaries similar to the ones modeled by your parents?

Parent boundaries now:

....

....

....

Parent boundaries then:

....

....

....

....

Boundaries with my children:

....

....

....

....

....

....

6. Sibling Boundaries

If you have siblings, consider and list the boundaries you need in these relationships. How, if at all, are they different from your boundaries with your parents?

....

....

....

....

....

....

7. Nonverbal Behavior with Children

In what way would you adjust your nonverbal behavior when refusing an unreasonable request of your or any child, compared to a request made by a coworker?

....

....

....

8. Yours, Mine, Ours

If you have a sibling(s), use the following Venn diagram to help you explore the boundaries of your individuality. Label one circle for you, and the other for your sibling. Add more circles to the diagram for additional siblings, or use an extra sheet of paper if you have many siblings, as I do. Describe traits, activities, interests, etc. that are unique to you in your portion of the circle, then do the same for your siblings. In the portion of the circle(s) shared by all of your circles, list commonalities.

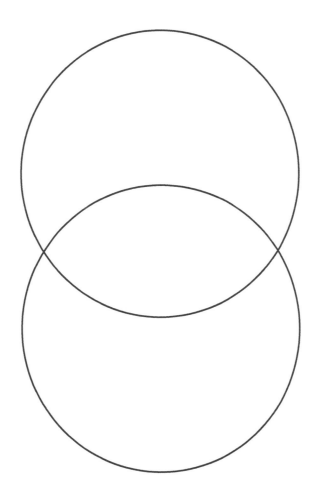

9. Boundary Contingency Plans: Parents

Write an assertive response to each of the following scenarios:

If my parent(s) criticize my choice in a romantic partner, then I will ....

....

....

If my parent(s) inappropriately compare me to a sibling, then I will ....

....

....

If my parent(s) insist that I stay with them for the holidays, although they know that this year I'm supposed to stay with my partner's family, then I will ....

....

....

10. Boundary Contingency Plans: Siblings

Write an assertive response to each of the following scenarios:

If my sibling ignores my calls, then I will ....

....

....

If my sibling borrows something without asking/with no intention of returning it, then I will ....

....

....

If my sibling insists I help them get a job and put together their résumé and cover letter, then I will ....

....

....

11. Boundary Contingency Plans: Children

Write an assertive response to each of the following scenarios:

If my child hits their sibling or another child, then I will _____

_____

_____.

If my child tells me they hate me, then I will _____

_____

_____.

If my child insists that they will only eat cake for breakfast, then I will ____

_____

_____.

12. Uh-oh

Consider a time when you were younger and got into trouble. How did your parents respond? Would you characterize their approach as passive, assertive, or aggressive?

_____

_____

_____

_____

_____

_____

_____

13. Square, Circle, Triangle, Square, Circle . . .

Is your current style of parenting similar to that of your parents? In what way are these patterns similar or different? What did you like and dislike about your parents' approach? What would you do differently?

....

....

....

....

....

....

....

....

....

14. What's the Problem?

What is the problem with using punishment when disciplining children? Note that I'm *not* talking about physical or corporal punishment; this is obviously inappropriate, aggressive, and harmful on physical and emotional levels. I'm referring to the operational conditioning definition of punishment: giving an undesirable consequence (like extra chores) or taking away something desirable (like electronics) to reduce an undesirable behavior (like hitting, yelling, or stealing).

....

....

....

....

....

CHAPTER FIVE

ASSERTIVENESS IN CLOSE RELATIONSHIPS

Until now, we've focused on assertiveness in relationships that we don't necessarily get to choose, like those with our coworkers, managers, customers, and even families. This chapter will discuss the particulars of being assertive in our close and voluntary relationships, specifically our romantic relationships and friendships.

Romantic Relationships

Are you someone who finds it hard to be yourself when you are dating someone? Are you suddenly quieter, not doing the things you love or spending time with the other people in your life? This could indicate poor boundaries in a relationship and a passive communication style. Maybe instead you have had a series of relationships that always seem filled with drama or arguments and you lose your cool, indicating a potential problem with respecting others' boundaries and using aggressive communication. Whatever the case, this chapter and the exercises included at the end will help you evaluate your relationship needs and improve the way you communicate to meet them.

A healthy romantic relationship can be difficult to maintain or even initiate without assertiveness. One particular challenge of being assertive in this kind of relationship involves your experiences in past relationships. Recall from chapter 1 that your past experiences and the outcome of previous attempts at assertiveness can shape your current communication patterns (see page 6). If a previous partner encouraged you to speak up and share your feelings, thoughts, and needs, then you may feel empowered and comfortable asserting yourself. If instead you had a partner who criticized you when you spoke, made you feel guilty for your thoughts or feelings, or even made you doubt your own thoughts or feelings—called gaslighting—then these experiences might have taught you that it is unsafe or pointless to speak up.

Fear can also prevent you from asserting yourself. You could have a fear of abandonment, that your partner will leave you if you do speak up. It could also be fear of failing in a relationship. This can be particularly strong after a bad breakup or a divorce, and it may unconsciously motivate you to stay in a toxic relationship or adopt a communication pattern that keeps the relationship going but doesn't serve you. Or maybe it's another kind of fear. Take some time and think about what is stopping you from asserting yourself in your romantic relationships. The first three exercises at the end of this chapter will help you address these barriers.

Several issues might come up in a relationship that will require you to be assertive with your partner. One common issue for cohabitating couples is division of household chores. If you find yourself always taking out the trash, doing laundry, vacuuming, or cleaning the bathroom while your partner doesn't take on any of this work, resentment toward your partner can build and then release in passive-aggressive or even aggressive ways. Assertive communication here might involve making direct requests of your partner to assist with chores. If your partner still doesn't contribute, you may need to escalate to a wider conversation about how the situation makes you feel and what you need. This would be a good time to practice using an "I statement."

Another issue involves the balance of how much time you spend with or on your significant other, compared to how much you spend on yourself. Maybe you have a partner who wants you to spend all your time with them. This might cross your physical boundary of time or cause conflict when you want to spend some time alone or even with other people in your support network. Here you might have to reinforce your boundaries by communicating what they are and why they are there, such as what need they help you satisfy.

Finances are still another issue requiring assertiveness. Money can be a touchy subject in a relationship, due to each person's rational or irrational associations with it. If you are struggling to support yourself, you might feel uncomfortable in relationships where your partner often makes plans to go to fancy restaurants, take romantic getaways, or pursue other expensive ventures that indirectly communicate an expectation to spend that feels beyond your means. Assertiveness might look like setting boundaries around how much you can spend monthly on dates, or saying no to activities *before* you start to feel exhausted financially. Alternatively, you might have a partner who frequently complains about not having money and might ask for your help paying for things, but then you see them spend $300 on a pair of shoes. This might make you feel taken advantage of or angry, and you would need to address this through assertiveness.

Regardless of the situation, it is important to have conversations early in the relationship about expectations, boundaries, and needs. Of course, you do not need to address all these things on the first date. You can allow the conversations to occur organically; as things come up, speak up. Even if you have been in a relationship for a while and there are years of precedent or years when you have been passive, it's not too late to change. A direct conversation about your current relationship patterns, why they are not working for you, and what you need or would like to do differently will be needed. Remember that asserting yourself is not a one-time conversation in any relationship, but an ongoing process of discussing new situations as they come up and advocating for yourself. If you and your partner get into a repetitive loop of these conversations without much change, or if the conversations end with a lot of negative feelings, then it might be time to see if a couples' therapist can help.

Sample Script

It's Saturday, and you and your partner both have the day off. The house is a mess; dishes are in the sink, the laundry basket is overflowing, and every counter and tabletop is littered with miscellaneous paperwork, old takeout containers, etc. You get out of bed with the plan of tackling some of this, and you notice that your partner is getting dressed to leave the house.

YOU: I need your help cleaning the house.

PARTNER: I can't right now. I have to meet up with Alex.

YOU: Okay. When will you be able to help?

PARTNER: Ugh, maybe not until next week. I really just want to relax today. Besides, it doesn't look that bad in here.

YOU: I am feeling overwhelmed because of how messy everything is right now. I really need your help. We are not going to have food to eat or clothes to wear this week if we wait. After your lunch with Alex, can you help me clean for a couple hours? Or maybe we could divide the chores?

Helpful Phrases

"This is not me vs. you. We're a team and I'd like us to work on this together."

"It seems like we might have a different viewpoint or need related to X. Let's talk about this."

"I've been struggling with the way we've been communicating and need to make some changes."

Dating and New Relationships

Dating can be nerve-racking, especially first dates. It can feel a bit like you're going to a job interview—but it doesn't have to. It can even be *fun*!

Asserting yourself in a new relationship is important. People might be more tempted to avoid assertiveness in a new relationship out of fear of jeopardizing it before it begins. This taps into impression management—the process of wanting to give off a good impression and acting in a way to make another person like you.

But here's the problem: What's the point of someone liking you if they always cross your boundaries or ignore your needs, and you can't be yourself with them? Holding back might help you get into a relationship, but it may not be a relationship you really want or will feel fulfilled in.

Different expectations for the longevity of the relationship is a typical issue in a very new relationship. Does the other person just want to hook up, or are they looking for something more serious? Their wish might be inconsistent with what you want. Questions like "What are you looking for?" or "What do you want out of a relationship right now?" will help you evaluate these expectations.

Ghosting—the phenomenon of someone abruptly vanishing from a relationship without explanation—is another common issue. Whether you have been ghosted or have done the ghosting, not having an answer to why the relationship ended can be mentally exhausting. It can also bring up a lot of negative and irrational beliefs about yourself ("I'm not good enough" or "I can't handle this") or about others ("People are mean" or "Men/women can't be trusted"). Ghosting sometimes reinforces a pattern of passivity and conflict avoidance. The more you avoid conflict, the more you feel you need to avoid it, building it up as an insurmountable obstacle. However, there might be times when ghosting and avoidance are realistically appropriate. For example, if you don't feel safe in a new relationship, it can give you a way out that might feel safer than confrontation and provide a method of defending your boundaries.

If you're reading this, you are probably working to change how you communicate in relationships. Luckily, the fact that you're going through this process is perfectly acceptable to discuss with a new partner. Saying something like "In the past, I have felt my relationships were unequal, and I've been working on learning to assert myself and my needs more" can be helpful. This lets the other person know your boundaries and where you are coming from, and it also makes your expectation of having open and honest communication clear. It may also invite your partner to feel comfortable asserting themselves, or to provide you with feedback about how you are asserting yourself.

Sample Script

It's been a while since you have dated anyone, but now you feel ready for a new relationship and look forward to settling down. You sign up for a dating app and get a message from Sam. You are drawn to their profile, and in chatting you find that you have a lot in common, but so far you are not sure what they want out of a relationship.

> YOU: I really like talking to you and think we have a lot in common. Before things go too far, can you tell me what are you looking for in a relationship now?

> SAM: I just want to have fun.

> YOU: Does that mean you are looking for a casual romance, or that you're not interested in a serious relationship?

> SAM: Yeah, I'm not ready for anything serious.

> YOU: This unfortunately isn't going to work out, then. I'm looking for more of a commitment.

"Right now, I'm looking for X in a relationship."

"I'm not ready for this level of commitment/physical intimacy."

Friends

We owe a lot to our friends. While relationships with others, like coworkers and romantic partners, may enter and exit your world, a good friendship can span a large part of your life. This can make our friends feel like anchors who stabilize us during life's transitions. As we grow up and enter adulthood, friends can fill in some of the gaps from our home lives. No siblings? Your friendships will teach you about sharing with others. Feel unsupported at home? Friends can provide much-needed love and support. Think you're weird and don't belong? Friends can normalize those feelings. Get a new job? They are there to celebrate. Getting married? They'll pop the champagne with you. Having a kid? They may be willing to organize a baby shower, don pastel colors, and play inane games with a bunch of your extended family and coworkers. Going through a breakup or divorce? Friends are still by your side, ready to lend an ear or a shoulder and take your phone away from you so you don't text your ex.

Your friends do a lot for you, and you do a lot for them—out of reciprocity, sincerity, a sense of obligation, a fear of losing each other, or simple loyalty and commitment.

The term "friendship" describes a range of relationships of different depths and circumstances. You can have good friends—true gems like the ones I just described. Then you may have some okay friends, acquaintances, friends of friends, or friends who make you question how real the friendship is over time. Compared to other relationships, friendships might have fewer boundaries in some areas. For example, we might be comfortable sharing more of ourselves, our thoughts, our time, and our possessions with friends. We might also have more boundaries in some areas; we might expect more support, honesty, and give-and-take.

Your boundaries and how assertively you might need to defend them will vary in part by the degree of the friendship. You will likely need to assert yourself more with a new friend, or an acquaintance who doesn't know you or your boundaries very well. Take some time to think about your friend-related needs and what your boundaries are in a friendship, keeping in mind that these might vary with different friends. Some common issues may come up in friendships that require assertiveness.

You've been good friends with someone for years. You might typically hang out once a week, constantly text each other, and play video games together on the weekend. Then, life changed, and now you can't do these things—at least not in the same way. Maybe you just had a kid, you moved a little farther away, or you got accepted into a rigorous graduate school program. These life transitions may require you to redraw the boundaries in your friendship. This might look like telling your friend that you need to meet up less frequently, or that you want to swap out some of the usual all-night bar hangs for a meetup at a kid-friendly restaurant during the day.

The following sample script is an additional example of a situation that would require you to assert yourself with a friend.

Sample Script

Your friend is getting married and having a bachelor/bachelorette weekend blowout in Las Vegas, and they invite you to come. Your friend is asking everyone to pay $3,000 to cover the cost of the hotel, dinners, shows, and bar/club hopping. Oh, and you have to pay your own airfare, which costs roughly $600. You just started a new job and can't afford to spend thousands of dollars or take time off from work this early in the job.

YOU: I won't be able to go to your bachelor/ette party.

FRIEND: What? You have to come! It will be so much fun.

YOU: I'm sure it will be a lot of fun and I'd love to be able to go, but I can't.

FRIEND: Oh, come on. It's Vegas, baby! Why can't you?

YOU: I just started a job and honestly can't afford it right now. I'm excited for you, though, and I know it'll be a lot of fun.

Helpful Phrases

"I don't want to do X. I'd rather we did Y instead."

"Sometimes when we talk, I feel like I am put in a role of listening and supporting you, but don't feel like I am getting the same in return. I'd like our conversations to feel more balanced."

"I really value our friendship, but I won't put up with _____."

"I know texting is convenient and quick, but I also like talking on the phone. Can I call you later?"

The following exercises will help you identify your boundaries in romantic relationships and friendships and practice assertively responding to various situations. As you go through the exercises, reflect on your current and past partners or friends.

EXERCISES

1. Relationship Blocks

List what stops you from asserting yourself in your romantic relationships. This might include situations, fears, thoughts, or feelings that are rational, like previous experiences of being shut down in a similar situation or concern that you might hurt someone's feelings, or irrational, as if your voice doesn't matter or a disaster will ensue if you disagree.

2. Relationship Blocks 2

Let's address the barriers you listed in the first exercise. The approach you use will vary depending on how reality-based the barrier is. For your rational reasons, try using problem-solving strategies to identify actionable steps you can take to work on these barriers. Use this space to start problem solving.

3. Relationship Blocks 3

If you question how rational some of your reasons are—and think they may be based more on feelings, fears, and unhelpful beliefs than on facts or past experiences—try this exercise.

Complete the sentence with the first thing that comes to your mind: *I can't stand up to my partner because* ....

....

Look at what you wrote and play the role of a lawyer. Using the space provided, come up with a list of evidence that supports this explanation, followed by a list of evidence that refutes it. Then, weigh the evidence as a lawyer might to determine if your explanation is true.

Which side has more evidence? If your explanation is more true than false, engage in problem solving as discussed in exercise 2. If it is not true, rewrite the sentence here:

I think/feel that I can't stand up to my partner because of ....

....

but really ....

....

EVIDENCE FOR	EVIDENCE AGAINST

4. Romantic Boundaries

Make a list of things you will not put up with in a romantic relationship.

5. Boundary Contingency Plans: Romantic Relationships

Write an assertive response to each of the following scenarios:

If I catch my significant other lying to me, then I will ....

....

....

If I feel that my partner and I aren't doing enough things together, I will ....

....

....

If my partner criticizes my close friend, I will ....

....

....

If my partner always expects me to plan a date, I can ....

....

....

If, on a date with someone new, they ask me to meet their parents and I am
uncomfortable doing that, I will ....

....

....

6. Boundary Contingency Plans: Friends

Write an assertive response to each of the following scenarios:

If my friend constantly shows up late for our plans, then I will ....

....

....

....

....

If a friend borrowed money from me and hasn't returned it yet, I will ....

....

....

....

....

If my friend always ditches me to be with their significant other, I will ....

....

....

....

....

7. Friendship Boundaries

Make a list of things you will not put up with in a friendship. How is this list different from the list you made in exercise 4?

8. Body Language

You see a couple on the street arguing. Can you tell how they're each communicating by observing their nonverbal communication? What would aggressive body language look like? What about passive body language? Assertive?

Aggressive: ....

....

Passive: ....

....

Assertive: ....

....

9. Expressing Affection Assertively

You are in a new relationship and you are at a point where you want to engage in physical displays of affection. What is an assertive approach for bringing this up to your partner?

....

....

....

....

....

....

10. Ghosted?

You had an amazing date with someone you really like. You've texted them to arrange another date, but it's been a week and you haven't heard anything. You're not sure if you've been ghosted or if they are just busy. Write out an assertive text you could send.

....

....

....

....

11. Terrible First Date

Consider your worst first-date experience. Describe why it was so bad. Do you think assertiveness could have had a positive impact? What could assertiveness have looked like in this situation?

....

....

....

....

....

....

....

....

12. Toxic Friends

How do you know it is time to leave a friendship? If you have had to leave a friendship before, how did you do it? Would you use the same approach now?

13. Frustrating Friend-of-a-Friend

Your best friend gave you a ticket to a concert for a band you love, and they also invited their other friend whom you can't stand. What do you do?

_____

_____

_____

_____

_____

_____

_____

_____

_____

14. You Are at a Party

How might you act differently if you were going to a party with your significant other instead of your friend? What could this change in behavior mean?

_____

_____

_____

_____

_____

_____

15. Friendly Friends

You are pretty sure a new friend is flirting with you, and you are not interested in them romantically. How could you assertively address this with them?

CHAPTER SIX

ASSERTIVENESS OUT IN THE WORLD

So far, we've covered assertiveness at work, with family, and in close personal relationships. Now, let's branch out to discuss how you can apply your skills to your interactions with the rest of the world. In this final chapter we will discuss how assertiveness can help you talk to strangers, make new friends, get what you want as a customer, and talk to people who might be a little intimidating, like doctors, plumbers, car salespeople, mechanics, and more.

It's Okay to Talk to Strangers

I get it—people are busy. I live in New York City, and sometimes it feels like everyone is zooming around like bees in a hive. Humans are social creatures, and we thrive on connection. It's okay to break through the barrier of "being busy" and get to know people. Besides, being busy and being social are not opposites; you can be both. You can spare the 30 seconds or less it takes to say hi to a neighbor, smile at the people you pass on the street on your way to work, or even hold a door open for someone. These little interactions make us feel connected and that we're part of the world. They can also help us get out of ourselves and step away from our worries or point of view to see the bigger picture in life.

And let's face it: You're going to need to talk to strangers. You will eventually get lost and need to ask for directions, or you'll need to ask a store clerk where the toilet brushes are. You might see someone wearing the perfect purse that you have been looking for your whole life and need to know where they got it.

Aside from needing to talk to strangers, you are also going to want to talk to new people sometimes. Maybe you moved to a new city for a job and want to make friends, or you are attracted to someone and want to ask them out on date. It's useful to address the possible awkwardness or discomfort of talking to strangers because it's a great opportunity to practice your assertiveness skills! The overall interaction will likely be short and you probably won't ever see these people again, so who cares if it's awkward, your face turns red, or you mix up your words? All practice is good practice and can help teach us about what works for us.

Sample Script

You've just injured your knee and are trying to take the train to work. As luck would have it, there are no open seats. You can either hold on to the pole and hope you make it to your office without worsening your injury, or you can ask someone to give up their seat.

YOU: Would you be willing to trade places with me? I've injured my knee and need to sit down.

PERSON ON THE TRAIN: [Wearing headphones, appears to be ignoring you.]

YOU: [Leaning in a little closer, making eye contact.] Excuse me. I've injured my knee and need to sit down. Would you be willing to trade places with me?

PERSON ON THE TRAIN: Sure.

"Excuse me. I'm looking for X. Could you help me?"

"I'm trying to get to X, but I seem to be lost. Do you know where it is?"

"I really like your _____ ! Where did you get it?"

Making New Friends

Repeated contact with a former stranger, an acquaintance, or a classmate can build a foundation of familiarity and likability—necessary components for turning these casual relationships into long-term friendships. This transformation won't happen, however, without assertiveness. It takes assertiveness to put yourself out there, engage with people, invite them out, and follow up on plans like meeting up for coffee or going to a party. Sure, you could do these things passively or aggressively, but what would those outcomes be? It's hard to say, but it probably wouldn't be a new friendship—especially at the level you want.

Assertively socializing to make new friends involves assertive listening, paying attention to what people say, reflecting common interests, and extending invitations. Finding someone you want to socialize with could be easy, but finding someone you can have a longer conversation with can get tricky. One common piece of advice is to socialize while doing an activity you already enjoy, like playing pool, browsing a bookstore, or attending a community event. You will likely already share a common interest with other people there, so you've got that first step out of the way. Now comes the hard part: striking up a conversation with a stranger. Luckily, your common interest gives you a natural discussion topic!

Socializing with people in a group can be a whole different ball game. Have you ever found yourself at a party or another social gathering where you don't know anyone else and mostly everyone is already talking in groups? It can be intimidating to try to break into a group conversation, but your assertive skills can come in handy here as well. If you can stand firm, make eye contact with someone in the group, use active listening, and then respond or add to something that they are discussing, you can find your way in. After that, introduce yourself and learn more about the person you're talking to, and then move on to the other group members. The conversation may also not continue, and that's okay, too—you'll just have to find other people to meet.

Acting assertively from the beginning can set the tone for the whole friendship. It communicates that you value directness, honesty, and respect, and also indirectly communicates how you want your friends to talk to you and treat you. This can help new friends better understand your opinions on issues and what your interests are, instead of lacking clarity about what you want or expect as you expand your friend network even more.

Making friends is a vulnerable process, much like dating. You are revealing that you have positive feelings for another person and that you want them to be part of your life. Reaching out to the people you want to be friends with can therefore feel uncomfortable, and that's okay. There is no perfect way of making friends. Chances are that if you *have* some friends already, you've done it successfully before. Consider how you got those friendships going, and give yourself some credit for having some relationship-building skills. Maybe you asked to exchange contact information after an initial conversation and a decision that you do want to be friends with this person. You might have made plans then to do something soon. After that it's a matter of following up, having fun during hangouts, listening assertively to the other person, and building a mutual give-and-take relationship.

Here is a sample script of what taking the first step in making new friends might look like.

Sample Script

You've just joined a pool league with the hope of making some new friends who also enjoy shooting pool. You are currently playing against someone, and after a fun game and pleasant conversation, you decide to assert yourself.

YOU: I had a lot of fun playing with you tonight. Have you ever played at X venue before?

POTENTIAL FRIEND: No, is it any good?

YOU: I love it. The tables are cheap and the music is always good. Would you want to check it out with me sometime in the next couple of weeks?

POTENTIAL FRIEND: Yeah, that sounds good.

YOU: Great. Let's exchange numbers. That way you can let me know what day or time works for you.

"Would you like to hang out sometime?"

"I'm planning on doing [some shared interest]. Do you want to come?"

"It was great meeting you tonight. Would you be interested in doing this again sometime?"

"Let me give you my number."

Being a Customer

If you are a customer at a store, you're there because they have something you need or want. Sometimes it can be as simple as walking in, getting what you came for, and leaving, all without much interaction. On other occasions, you may not be able to find what you're looking for, it may be the kind of store where you can't just grab what you want and go, or you need to talk to customer service. You'll need to speak up to get what you want.

Odds are you've been in one of these situations at least once in your life. Maybe you've needed to return something that's broken or an atrocious gift from a random relative. Perhaps you grabbed something that was on sale, but when the cashier rang it up, it scanned at the original price. Or maybe you ordered food through a delivery service, and it's now been over an hour with no delivery person in sight and no word from the restaurant.

So what do you do? Do you just accept these situations, take the loss, and move on, or do you assert yourself and get your needs met? To some, it may seem like a trade-off between being rude or a bother and trying to get what you want. But it is not rude to assert yourself, and there are real benefits to being assertive as a customer. For example, speaking up to a salesclerk about your item not ringing up at the discounted price could save you money. Expressing your needs to customer service and getting something returned could bring you peace of mind as you cross that off your to-do list.

Compare these actions now with being passive or aggressive. Taking a passive approach—where you do not speak up and make your needs known to the employees who can actually do something about them—is likely not going to lead to any positive outcomes. If instead you're being too aggressive with a customer service representative or delivery person, yelling and demanding that something be done a certain way, then they may not want to help you get what you need. As Grandma always said, you catch more flies with honey than with vinegar.

In chapter 3, I discussed being assertive with customers (see page 59). Though the roles are now reversed, many of the things to consider remain the same.

1. Respect the employee and their place of business. If you've ever worked retail or any other customer-facing job, then you know how difficult it can be. This is especially true when a customer is being disrespectful or demanding things that you cannot give them. Now that you're the customer, treat the employee with the same respect you'd want in this situation. That being said . . .

2. Respect yourself and your interests. You need something done, and the employee is the person who can help you. You do not need to acquiesce or tolerate poor service just for the sake of being polite, especially if it means your needs are not met.

3. Be consistent. If they tell you that something is not on sale, but you know for sure that it is, you don't have to back down immediately. You are free to assert yourself and request that they check the shelf or elevate the issue to a manager, while remaining respectful and courteous, of course.

Sample Script

You are trying to buy a new pair of shoes for work. You find a pair that would be great, but you can't find your size. The store is busy, but you spot a store associate and ask them to check if there is a pair in your size in the back room. It's been 15 minutes and you see the same associate sipping a soda and casually talking to a coworker. You could just let it go, be passive, and chalk it up as a loss, but you use this as an opportunity to assert yourself instead, and follow up with him.

YOU: Excuse me. Were you able to find these shoes in a size 8 in the back of the store?

STORE ASSOCIATE: Oh, I'm sorry. I totally got sidetracked and didn't check.

YOU: That's understandable. It's pretty busy in here today. Are you still able to check for me?

STORE ASSOCIATE: Sure.

YOU: Great, thank you.

Helpful Phrases

"Excuse me, I need help finding X. Could you tell me where it is?"

"This price is different than what is being advertised. Could you check that the posted price is correct?"

"I'd like to return this. When I got the product home and opened the box, it was damaged."

Communicate with Doctors, Plumbers, and More

If you are being treated by a doctor or hiring a plumber, a mechanic, or another professional, you are still technically a customer and will likely find the previous section useful. However, communicating with and asserting yourself to people who provide a professional service is a little different. These are people usually in a position of authority, and they also likely have much more expertise in their field than you do. These factors might make people less inclined to assert themselves with these professionals.

Also, consider these professions. We are likely not seeking them out just for fun. If you are going to a doctor, you are probably sick. If you're calling a plumber, you could be dealing with some literal shit. If you are going to a mechanic, your car's not in good shape. These are stressful times, and since these situations could all have pretty severe consequences for our health or our finances, it's hard to trust someone with these things. When we're stressed, we're also more likely to feel overwhelmed and either give in to passivity by giving up, or become angry and react aggressively.

In my work as a therapist, my job is to help my clients using the skills and knowledge I've acquired. As a professional, I'll readily admit that I don't have all the answers, and nor am I perfect. I encourage my clients to challenge me, correct me if I misheard something, and ask as many questions as they need. This ultimately helps me help them. I often hear about people not speaking up to a doctor because they feel stupid or don't want to be labeled a "problem patient." I've never perceived my clients this way. It doesn't matter if they completely disagree with me or with my assessment. If they are asking me questions or challenging me, I see them asserting themselves, and I am proud of them. It also shows me that they are committed to themselves and to making sure they can get the best service I am capable of providing.

Some people are taught not to question medical professionals due to things like the power differential, having been taught not to question authority, or simply not knowing what types of questions to ask. It's especially important to assert yourself in a medical setting, however, because it helps you make the most informed decision about your care. For example, you should ask about what your treatment will look like, including possible side effects or alternatives to treatment, so you have clear expectations for how your treatment will progress and learn about other options if the initial efforts do not work.

The next Helpful Phrases section includes many things that you can say to a medical professional to appropriately advocate for yourself. Many of these phrases can also be easily reworked for use with professionals in other fields as well.

These professionals rely on us as much as we rely on them, so the relationship should be mutually beneficial. Doctors need patients. Plumbers need leaky pipes. Mechanics need broken cars. It is important to let these professionals know exactly what you want and why you want it, and it is just as important that you know how they arrived at their recommendations. These professionals should be able to justify their decisions, as it keeps them accountable. Also, if you need to get a second opinion, you can verify the thinking of the first professional, and that can give you peace of mind if there is agreement or knowledge of alternative options if they disagree. This allows us to feel greater trust in the interaction. It is essential to give professionals as much information as possible and make sure that you are both fully on board with any solution. This can alleviate any suffering down the road caused by your not expressing your concerns.

Sample Script

You need a new car. You're at a dealership and see a car that you like. The sticker price is $2,000 more than the MSRP you saw online.

CAR SALESMAN: I see you're looking at this car. You've got great taste! It's one of our best models.

YOU: Thank you. Unfortunately, the sticker price is $2,000 more than I am willing to spend.

CAR SALESMAN: There's plenty of other models we can show you that may be in your price range.

YOU: This car has a lot of things that I need, like four-wheel drive, ample seating in the back, and high safety ratings, so I am interested in this model. Is it possible to reduce the price by $2,000?

Helpful Phrases

"My budget for this is X. Are you able to stick within that?"

"What are the risks associated with this medication/procedure?"

"What is the plan if there is a complication or adverse reaction?"

"How did you arrive at this diagnosis?"

"What can I do to help with my care?"

"This is not what we agreed on."

EXERCISES

1. Stranger No Danger

Practice talking to strangers in safe situations this week. Aim for brief chitchat conversations with at least two different strangers in typical destinations during your week, like the grocery store, the coffee shop, or the train. Describe how this went. Was it easy? Harder than you expected? How do you think you were perceived? If you were to do it again, what would you change?

_____

_____

_____

_____

_____

_____

_____

_____

2. Boundary Contingency Plans: Strangers

Write an assertive response to each of the following scenarios:

If I am in the checkout line at a store and someone cuts in front of me, I will

_____

_____

_____

_____

If my taxi driver is making me uncomfortable by asking me personal questions, I will ....

....

....

If I'm riding the train and a stranger is stepping on my bag, I will ....

....

....

3. Boundary Contingency Plans: Making Friends

Write an assertive response to each of the following scenarios:

If I meet someone at an event that I get along with well, I will ....

....

....

If I'm at a party and I don't know anyone, I will ....

....

....

If a new friend crosses one of my boundaries and we cannot compromise, I will

....

....

....

....

4. Boundary Contingency Plans: As a Customer

Write an assertive response to each of the following scenarios:

If a salesperson is rude to me, I will _____

_____

_____.

If I ask a store employee for help, but they do not follow through, I will _____

_____

_____.

If I am getting angry because a salesperson is talking over me, I will _____

_____

_____.

5. Boundary Contingency Plans: Professionals

Write an assertive response to each of the following scenarios:

If my doctor quickly diagnoses my condition and starts to leave the room before I have time to ask questions, I will _____

_____

_____.

If the plumber tells me the problem is much larger and more expensive than they originally thought, I will _____

_____

_____.

If I don't understand why a professional is recommending a particular solution, I will _____

_____

_____.

6. Making Friends

Consider the last friend you made. How did the relationship get started? Who initiated the friendship? How did you feel in those initial interactions? What made you want to be friends with them?

7. Finding Friends

As we discussed, a good place for making friends is at a place you like to go or while doing an activity that you enjoy. If you were trying to make friends now, where would you go or what would you do?

8. I Didn't Order This

If you are at a restaurant and the waiter brings you the wrong order, how comfortable would you be speaking up? Describe why. List passive, aggressive, and assertive responses to this.

9. Practice and Party

It's Friday night and you were invited to go to a party by an acquaintance you hope becomes a closer friend. You decide to go to the party, even though you only know that one person, thinking "Hey, it will be a great opportunity to talk to people." Good for you! Admittedly, you feel a bit like an awkward wallflower at first. What would assertive and confident body language look like? What would you do?

10. No Thanks

You recently met a friend-of-a-friend, and they have since followed you on social media and reached out to you to hang out. You don't feel that you have much common interest with this person, and aren't really interested in becoming friends with them. What do you do?

11. Stranger Discomfort

In what situations would you genuinely feel uncomfortable talking to a stranger? Make a list. Consider the source of your discomfort. Do you feel that this discomfort is rational and thus you should avoid talking to these strangers, or do you feel the discomfort is irrational and is something you want to change?

12. Assertiveness and Age

How do you feel that the age difference between you and the professional trying to help you affects the interaction? What if your doctor is older than you? What if they're younger? Would this make it easier or harder for you to assert yourself if you disagreed with them? Why or why not?

13. Treatment Decisions

Your doctor has discussed two different options for treating a condition you have. With the information you have received, neither option seems more attractive than the other. What questions would you ask your doctor to help you make your decision?

14. How Much?

You just got a bill from an electrician that is much higher than the amount agreed upon to fix your bathroom vent. Your initial reaction is anger. What would an assertive approach look like in this situation?

....

....

....

15. Practice Makes Progress

Identify three current situations where you can practice being assertive. Why is it important to assert yourself in these situations? What could you gain by being assertive? List the steps you would need to take. After you have completed these, describe how it went.

Situation #1

....

....

....

....

Situation #2

....

....

....

....

Situation #3

....

....

....

....

FINAL WORD: KEEP PRACTICING

As you continue your journey toward assertiveness, remember to breathe, practice as much as you can, and be kind to yourself. You are trying something new, and it has the power to change your life. That's not a small thing! As you practice, strive for progress, not perfection. Incremental progress can build big things, and, if you are consistent, you'll see the change you are looking for. Perfectionism, on the other hand, can build a pressure so intense that it stops you from ever taking a step, or destroys the motivation needed to help you reach your goals. Keep persisting in your practice until you are able to consistently articulate your needs, set clear boundaries, and be your own best advocate.

Also, remember that assertiveness starts with being assertive with yourself. Leave the negative self-judgment and criticism at the door. This aggressive self-communication is counterproductive to your goal of learning to assert yourself and be your own best advocate. Be honest with yourself about what you want, what you need, and what boundaries are necessary to help you meet those needs. Be flexible. Also note that as you are learning to become more assertive, your thoughts about what you want or need might change—and that's okay. Give yourself room to grow and to learn about yourself. You got this.

RESOURCES

The Center for Nonviolent Communication. Need help identifying your needs? Check out their Needs Inventory.

"Fake It Till You Make It," a TED talk by Amy Cuddy about the importance of nonverbal communication and power posing.

Treating Alcohol Dependence: A Coping Skills Training Guide by Peter M. Monti, Ronald M. Kadden, Damaris J. Rohsenow, Ned L. Cooney, and David B. Abrams. This is a wonderful workbook that addresses assertiveness skills within the context of alcohol dependence issues (e.g., drink refusal, giving critical feedback, etc.).

NOTES

1. Bem, Sandra L. "The Measurement of Psychological Androgyny." *Journal of Consulting and Clinical Psychology* 42, no. 2 (1974): 155–162.
2. Sebanc, Anne M., Susan L. Pierce, Carol L. Cheatham, and Megan R. Gunnar. "Gendered Social Worlds in Preschool: Dominance, Peer Acceptance and Assertive Social Skills in Boys' and Girls' Peer Groups." *Social Development* 12, no. 1 (January 2003): 91–106.
3. Maloney, Mary E., and Patricia Moore. "From Aggressive to Assertive." *International Journal of Women's Dermatology* 6, no. 1 (January 2020): 46–49.
4. Leaper, Campbell, and Tara E. Smith. "A Meta-Analytic Review of Gender Variations in Children's Language Use: Talkativeness, Affiliative Speech, and Assertive Speech." *Developmental Psychology* 40, no. 6 (November 2004): 993–1027.
5. Mulac, Anthony, James J. Bradac, and Pamela Gibbons. "Empirical Support for the Gender-as-Culture Hypothesis." *Human Communication Research* 27, no. 1 (January 2001): 121–152.
6. Hofstede, Geert, Gert Jan Hofstede, and Michael Minkov. *Cultures and Organizations: Software of the Mind*. London and New York: McGraw Hill, 2010.
7. Holtgraves, Thomas. "Styles of Language Use: Individual and Cultural Variability in Conversational Indirectness." *Journal of Personality and Social Psychology* 73, no. 3 (September 1997): 624–637.
8. Burgoon, Judee K., Laura K. Guerrero, and Kory Floyd. *Nonverbal Communication*. New York: Routledge, 2016.
9. San Martin, Alvaro, Marwan Sinaceur, Amer Madi, Steve Tompson, William W. Maddux, and Shinobu Kitayama. "Self-Assertive Interdependence in Arab Culture." *Nature Human Behaviour* 2, no. 11 (2018): 830–837.
10. Sigler, Kathy, Ann Burnett, and Jeffrey T. Child. "A Regional Analysis of Assertiveness." *Journal of Intercultural Communication Research* 37, no. 2 (July 2008): 89–104.
11. Hollandsworth, James G., Jr. "Further Investigation of the Relationship between Expressed Social Fear and Assertiveness." *Behaviour Research and Therapy* 14, no. 1 (1976): 85–87.
12. Speed, Brittany C., Brandon L. Goldstein, and Marvin R. Goldfried. "Assertiveness Training: A Forgotten Evidence-Based Treatment." *Clinical Psychology: Science and Practice* 25, no. 1 (October 2017).

13. Abele, Andrea E., Nicole Hauke, Kim Peters, Eva Louvet, Aleksandra Szymkow, and Yanping Duan. "Facets of the Fundamental Content Dimensions: Agency with Competence and Assertiveness—Communion with Warmth and Morality." *Frontiers in Psychology* 7 (2016): 1810.

14. Bijstra, Jan O., Harke A. Bosma, and Sandy Jackson. "The Relationship between Social Skills and Psycho-Social Functioning in Early Adolescence." *Personality and Individual Differences* 16, no. 5 (1994): 767–776.

15. Shrestha, Pramen P., and Nancy Menzel. "Hispanic Construction Workers and Assertiveness Training." *Work* 49, no. 3 (2014): 517–522.

16. Speed, Goldstein, and Goldfried. "Assertiveness Training.

17. Eslami, Ahmad Ali, Leili Rabiei, Seyed Mohammad Afzali, Saeed Hamidizadeh, and Reza Masoudi. "The Effectiveness of Assertiveness Training on the Levels of Stress, Anxiety, and Depression of High School Students." *Iranian Red Crescent Medical Journal* 18, no. 1 (2016).

18. Lin, Yen-Ru, I-Shin Shiah, Yue-Cune Chang, Tzu-Ju Lai, Kwua-Yun Wang, and Kuei-Ru Chou. "Evaluation of an Assertiveness Training Program on Nursing and Medical Students' Assertiveness, Self-Esteem, and Interpersonal Communication Satisfaction." *Nurse Education Today* 24, no. 8 (November 2004): 656–665.

19. Parray, Waqar Maqbool, and Sanjay Kumar. "Impact of Assertiveness Training on the Level of Assertiveness, Self-Esteem, Stress, Psychological Well-Being and Academic Achievement of Adolescents." *Indian Journal of Health and Wellbeing* 8, no. 12 (2017): 1476–1480.

20. Animasahun, R. A., and O. O. Oladeni. "Effects of Assertiveness Training and Marital Communication Skills in Enhancing Marital Satisfaction among Baptist Couples in Lagos State, Nigeria." *Global Journal of Human Social Science Arts & Humanities* 12, no. 14 (2012): 342–351.

21. Parray Kumar. "Impact of Assertiveness Training on the Level of Assertiveness, Self-Esteem, Stress, Psychological Well-Being and Academic Achievement of Adolescents."

22. Abele, Hauke, Peters, et al. "Facets of the Fundamental Content Dimensions: Agency with Competence and Assertiveness.

23. Kuntze, Jeroen, Henk T. van der Molen, and Marise Ph. Born. "Big Five Personality Traits and Assertiveness Do Not Affect Mastery of Communication Skills." *Health Professions Education* 2, no. 1 (2016): 33–43.

24. Carney, Dana R., Amy J. C. Cuddy, and Andy J. Yap. "Power Posing: Brief Nonverbal Displays Affect Neuroendocrine Levels and Risk Tolerance." *Psychological Science* 21, no. 10 (September 2010): 1363–1368.

25. Center for Nonviolent Communication. "Needs Inventory." Last modified 2005. cnvc.org.

26. World Health Organization. "Global Strategy on Occupational Health for All: The Way to Health at Work." 1994. Who.int/occupational_health/globstrategy/en.

27. Butt, Aqsa, and Zahid Mahmood Zahid. "Effect of Assertiveness Skills on Job Burnout." *International Letters of Social and Humanistic Sciences* 63 (November 2015): 218–224.

28. Sarafino, Edward P., and Timothy W. Smith. *Health Psychology: Biopsychosocial Interactions.* Hoboken, NJ: John Wiley & Sons, 2014.

29. Amanatullah, Emily T., and Michael W. Morris. "Negotiating Gender Roles: Gender Differences in Assertive Negotiating Are Mediated by Women's Fear of Backlash and Attenuated When Negotiating on Behalf of Others." *Journal of Personality and Social Psychology* 98, no. 2 (2010): 256–267.

30. Amanatullah, Emily T., and Catherine H. Tinsley. "Punishing Female Negotiators for Asserting Too Much . . . or Not Enough: Exploring Why Advocacy Moderates Backlash against Assertive Female Negotiators." *Organizational Behavior and Human Decision Processes* 120, no. 1 (January 2013): 110–122.

31. Dansereau, Fred Jr., George Graen, and William J. Haga. "A Vertical Dyad Linkage Approach to Leadership within Formal Organizations: A Longitudinal Investigation of the Role Making Process." *Organizational Behavior and Human Performance* 13, no. 1 (February 1975): 46–78.

32. Berk, Laura E. *Development through the Lifespan.* 6th ed. Boston: Pearson, 2014.

33. Nakhaee, Samaneh, Seyyed Abolfazl Vagharseyyedin, Ehsan Afkar, and Maryam Salmani Mood. "The Relationship of Family Communication Pattern with Adolescents' Assertiveness." *Modern Care Journal* 14, no. 4 (2017).

INDEX

ABOUT THE AUTHOR

Shandelle Hether-Gray, MA, LMHC, is a licensed mental health counselor in New York City. She has worked with clients of all ages since 2012, helping them learn how to assert themselves in their personal and professional lives. She is trained in evidence-based therapies such as cognitive behavioral therapy, which she uses to treat anxiety, depression, and self-esteem issues. Outside of clinical practice, Shandelle is an adjunct professor in psychology, and she is passionate about neuroscience. She has presented at conferences and has been published in peer-reviewed journals, including *Neuroscience* and *Epilepsy & Behavior*.